Francis Poulenc

Sonata
for flute and piano

Revised edition, 1994

Edited by Carl B. Schmidt

Consulting editor: Patricia Harper (1994)
with historical introduction and editorial commentary in English, French and German.

This piece has been arranged for flute and orchestra by Lennox Berkeley;
score and parts are available on hire from the publisher.

CH01605

ISBN 978-0-7119-4398-8

Exclusive Distributors:
Hal Leonard
7777 West Bluemound Road
Milwaukee, WI 53213
Email: info@halleonard.com

Hal Leonard Europe Limited
42 Wigmore Street
Marylebone, London, W1U 2RY
Email: info@halleonardeurope.com

Hal Leonard Australia Pty. Ltd.
4 Lentara Court
Cheltenham, Victoria, 3192 Australia
Email: info@halleonard.com.au

Chester Music

Francis Poulenc first mentioned that he was writing a flute sonata in a letter to his friend, the baritone Pierre Bernac, dated 2 September [1952] in which he remarked, 'Momentarily I have abandoned the Sonata for Two Pianos for a Sonata for Flute which suddenly took shape at the Austerlitz station last Thursday.'[2] Confirmation of this was published in the October issue of *The Chesterian*, the official magazine of Chester Music, which stated: 'Francis Poulenc is at present writing a Sonata for Flute and Piano which, it is hoped, will be ready for publication early next year. The work is being specially composed for a well known American flautist, who will introduce it in the United States.'[3] Very possibly the 'well known American flautist' was Julius Baker, who at this time was about to leave his position as principal of the Chicago Symphony and return to New York for positions as a teacher at The Juilliard School and as a performer in the CBS Orchestra and the Bach Aria Group.[4] Three letters from Poulenc to his publisher R. Douglas Gibson at Chester indicate that he contemplated resuming the work over a period of years. In 1953 he wrote: 'I am just finishing my Sonata for Two Pianos. God knows if I will ever take up the Flute Sonata again because I am going to write a large opera for La Scala based on *The Dialogues of the Carmelites.'*[5] In 1955 he added, 'After the summer I hope to take up again my idea for a Sonata for Flute.' Finally, in early 1956, Poulenc wrote, 'Perhaps this summer I will finish the Sonata for Flute.'

It is not known if this 'early' sonata is directly related to the published sonata, but it is highly likely. In a letter dated 3 April 1956, Harold Spivacke, Chief of the Music Division of the Library of Congress acting in his joint capacity as spokesperson for the Coolidge Foundation at the Library of Congress, wrote to Poulenc offering a commission for a piece of chamber music for a festival to take place on 19–21 October 1956.[6] Although Spivacke proposed a piece for two pianos, he left Poulenc the option of a different sort of work providing it did not exceed six instruments. Poulenc responded in a letter dated 13 April [1956] declining the commission on the grounds that he was just finishing the orchestration of his opera and that the premiere in Milan was too close. Undeterred, Spivacke again offered the commission in a letter dated 9 May 1956. Poulenc delayed his response until August at which point he noted that his opera was in order and that he could now envision writing something. He suggested a Sonata for Flute and Piano, dedicated to the memory of Elizabeth Sprague Coolidge, and agreed to Spivacke's proposed terms of $750 and the gift of the original manuscript to the Library of Congress provided that he could reserve the premiere for the Strasbourg Festival in June 1957.

Apparently Jean-Pierre Rampal learned about the sonata in a phone call from Poulenc not long after the commission. In his autobiography Rampal recalled the occasion. 'Jean-Pierre,' said Poulenc: 'you know you've always wanted me to write a sonata for flute and piano? Well, I'm going to,' he said. 'And the best thing is that the Americans will pay for it! I've been commissioned by the Coolidge Foundation to write a chamber piece in memory of Elizabeth Coolidge. *I* never knew her, so I think the piece is yours.'[7]

Additional letters between Poulenc and Spivacke or his deputies consummated the agreement, and Poulenc wrote the work in Cannes, France between December of 1956 and March of 1957. In a letter to Bernac dated 8 March [1957], Poulenc called the Sonata a work with 'Debussyste' proportions. On 9 March 1957 Poulenc wrote to R. Douglas Gibson of his progress: 'The first two movements of the Sonata are complete. I am pleased with them. It is a question of an *Allegretto melancolico* and of a *Cantilena*. The finale will be an *Allegro giocoso.'* Poulenc must have completed the finale quickly, because on 7 June 1957, just eleven days before he and Rampal presented the world premiere at the Strasbourg Festival, he mailed the completed manuscript to the Library of Congress.[8] Initially Poulenc intended to come to the United States to perform the work at the Library and actually proposed a recital with the singer Alice Esty which would have included the second American performance of his song cycle *Le Travail du peintre*.[9] When he realized that this concert would be his only reason for

---

[1] Information contained in this introduction is taken from Carl B. Schmidt's A *Catalogue of the Music of Francis Poulenc (1899–1963)* (Oxford, England: Oxford University Press, forthcoming) and from Patricia Harper's articles 'A Fresh Look at Francis Poulenc's *Sonata for Flute and Piano,' The Flutist Quarterly* 17, No. 1 (1992): 8–23 and 'A Further Look at Francis Poulenc's *Sonata for Flute and Piano,' The Flutist Quarterly* 18, No. 2 (1993/94): 48–57. See also her letter to the editor in *The Flutist Quarterly* 17, No. 3 (1992): 7.

[2] See the unpublished letter in Paris, Bibliothèque Nationale, Manuscript Department. All letters by Poulenc quoted in this edition have been translated from the French by the editor.

[3] See vol. 27, no. 172 (Oct. 1952): 40.

[4] Private conversations between Harper and Baker (25 Aug. and 16 Oct. 1993).

[5] See Poulenc's unpublished letters of 23 April [1953], 17 June [1955], and 25 Feb. [1957] London, J. W. Chester Archive.

[6] For this and other letters between Poulenc, Spivacke, and members of the staff, see 'Music Division Old Correspondence' at the Library of Congress in Washington, D.C.

[7] Jean-Pierre Rampal, *Music, My Love: An Autobiography with Deborah Wise* (New York: Random House, 1989), pp. 125–6. For a similar, but not identical account, see Katherine Goll-Wilson, 'Jean-Pierre Rampal on Making Music,' *Flute Talk* 10 (May 1991): 9–13.

[8] The unofficial premiere was given on 17 June 1957. In Rampal's words: 'On the morning before the first performance, Poulenc called me. "Arthur Rubinstein is here," he said. "I've just talked to him, and he very much wants to hear my new sonata. The only trouble is, he has to leave tomorrow before the performance. Do you think you could come over right now and have just one more rehearsal?" "With pleasure," I replied. So the unofficial premiere . . . took place in a concert hall in Strasbourg with an audience of one — Arthur Rubinstein, sitting in the middle of the front row. The applause we received from him was as memorable as at any concert I have played.' See Rampal, *Music, My Love,* p. 128.

[9] See Poulenc's letter of 7 June [1957].

coming to America, he demurred and suggested that the American premiere be arranged with Rampal and his pianist Robert Veyron-Lacroix. The American premiere took place in the Coolidge Auditorium at the Library of Congress on 14 February 1958 and was, according to newspaper accounts and a letter from Spivacke to Poulenc, a rousing success.[10]

Between the world premiere and the American premiere Poulenc found time to introduce the sonata to the English-speaking world through the BBC, a forum he had used on numerous occasions dating back to the 1920s. On 16 January 1958 Poulenc played the work with the renowned English flutist Gareth Morris.[11] Since these early performances, and Poulenc was to give others before his death, the Sonata for Flute and Piano has become one of the most frequently-performed and well-loved flute sonatas in the entire repertoire.[12] In preparing this new edition, the editors hope not only to clarify many textual issues but also to supply sufficient documentation for those who wish to know more about the background of the work and the significant problems involved in editing it.

THE SOURCES

The following sources, with their numerical sigla, have been used in preparing this new edition.

1. Autograph draft score (United States: New York City, Pierpont Morgan Library, Frederich R. Koch Foundation 639). This manuscript was given by Poulenc to his personal physician and bears the inscription in Poulenc's hand 'Pour mon ange / gardien, le cher / Docteur Chevalier / tendrement / Poulenc / [rule].' The manuscript is dated 'Majestic / Cannes / Décembre / 56' after movement 1 and 'Majestic / Cannes / Décembre [1956] / Mars 57' after movement 3. Companion to Source 3.

2. Autograph presentation score (United States: Washington D.C., Library of Congress, ML29c. P78 no. 1 case). Sent by Poulenc on 7 June 1957 to satisfy terms of the Coolidge Foundation commission.

3. Autograph flute part (France: Private library of Jean-Pierre Rampal). Used in preparing for the first performance, 18 June 1957. Companion to Source 1.

4. Copyist's flute part (Great Britain: Private library of Gareth Morris). Used for the first English performance on the BBC and inscribed to Morris by Poulenc on 16 Jan. 1958. This manuscript bears the inscription 'Pour Monsieur Morris / qui joue si merveilleusement / cette Sonate / avec un bien amical / merci. / Fr. Poulenc / [rule] / 16/1/58' and 'Day of the first *Carmélites* / performance', both in Poulenc's hand.

5a. First printed score (5a^s) and part (5a^p)(London: J. & W. Chester, Ltd. (J. W. C. 1605)), © 1958; 'Printed in Denmark' and 'WILHELM HANSENS NODESTIK OG TRYK KØBENHAVN. 1958 PRINTED IN DENMARK'; 23p + [i]; 30cm and part 8p; marked 'The flute part has been revised by JEAN-PIERRE RAMPAL [sic]'. The so-called '16th edition', the most current at this writing, contains only the slightest variants when compared to the first edition, and does not represent, in the technical sense, a new edition. It is actually a photographic reprint with occasional minor alterations.

5b. Editions 2–16 printed by Chester: score (5b^s) and part (5b^p). For a description, see above.

6. Pulenk, F. Sonata dlya fleity i f-p. [Red. partii fleity Zh. Rampel']. M.: Muzgiz, 1966. [Poulenc, F. Sonata for Flute and Pianoforte. [Editor of the flute part J. Rampel [Jean-Pierre Rampal]], Edited by V. Zverev, Moscow: Muzgiz, 1966]. 24p (score), 8p (part); 29cm; 3,240 copies; 39 copecks. This edition, based on 5a$^{s\&p}$ above, has not been collated. (Copy in Library of Congress.)

7a. Two pages of minor corrections in Poulenc's hand sent by him to J. W. Chester before the printed score and part were published (Great Britain: London, J. W. Chester Archive).

7b. An uncorrected set of proofsheets for the flute part (Great Britain: London, J. W. Chester Archive).

8a. Sound recording made by Jean-Pierre Rampal and Francis Poulenc at the time of the first performance in Strasbourg (18 June 1957).

8b. Sound recording made by Gareth Morris and Francis Poulenc for a BBC broadcast, 16 January 1958. (Copy in the possession of Morris.)

8c. Sound recording made by Jean-Pierre Rampal and Francis Poulenc during June 1959 as part of the series 'Présence de la Musique Contemporaine' (Véga C 35 A 181; re-released by Wergo as WER 50004, ca. 1963). The recording engineer was Pierre Rosenwald.

---

[10] See Day Thorpe's review in *The Evening* Star (Washington D.C.), 19 Feb. 1958 and Spivacke's letter of 24 Feb. 1958 in which he wrote: 'I am writing to tell you that the performance by Messrs. Rampal and Veyron-La Croix of your Sonata for Flute and Piano was a great success. The audience reaction was most enthusiastic, and I want you to know that we in the Music Division enjoyed it immensely.' A recording of this performance was sent to Poulenc with a copy retained by the Library of Congress.

[11] A tape of this performance, discarded by the BBC and now in the possession of M Morris, was consulted by the editors for this edition.

[12] For a detailed list of recordings including those by Poulenc, see Francine Bloch, *Phonographies Francis Poulenc 1928–1982* (Paris: Bibliothèque Nationale, 1984), pp. 186–90. See especially the two recordings made with Rampal in 1957 and 1959, and a third made at the Festival de Menton with Christian Lardé on 3 July 1962. In a letter to Gibson dated 14 Nov. [1957], Poulenc wrote of the first, 'I am happy to tell you that the recording of the Sonata for Flute [and Piano] is excellent.'

Relationship of the Sources and Missing Sources

In his autobiography, Jean-Pierre Rampal recounts that Poulenc, while in the midst of rehearsals for the Paris production of *Dialogues des Carmélites* (first given 18 June 1957), repeatedly summoned him to his 5 rue de Médicis apartment to play through the sonata as it grew.[13] Rampal makes clear that upon first sight: 'The first movement seemed disjointed, and there wasn't much of a theme or direction. The ideas came and went, but had no real coherence. And some of the fingering was impossible. I said so.' On a second occasion Rampal reported, 'I saw that his ideas were more coherent this time, but still far from finished.' Apparently Poulenc sent him off with some scraps of music to 'see if it's playable.' These meetings continued and Rampal noted: 'I did change a few phrases here and there and gave Francis some ideas as to how the work should hang together ... but I simply couldn't see where the piece was going — and was very much afraid Francis couldn't either. Yet he became more confident, and slowly but surely the Sonata for Flute and Piano took its final shape.'

Unfortunately, none of the manuscript fragments referred to above by Rampal has survived, and the earliest known written record of the Sonata is the rough piano score which Poulenc marked 'monstre Brouillon' on the first page (Source 1). This manuscript shows numerous signs of composition and clearly represents an early stage of the work in Poulenc's conception. It contains various cancelled measures, and the primary accompanimental figure in the first movement was to undergo considerable revision before the work was published.

The flute part in Poulenc's hand (Source 3), which Rampal indicates was used to prepare for the Strasbourg premiere, follows Source 1 in many particulars (dynamics, written-out trills, octave transpositions, cancelled passages, location of rehearsal numbers, etc.). It would appear that Rampal made changes to this part probably while rehearsing with Poulenc for the premiere because his additions often revise details written by Poulenc. This part is not the one from which either Source 4 or the printed scores (Sources $5a^{s\&p}$ & $5b^{s\&p}$) was copied.

The only manuscript fair copy of the work is Source 2, the exemplar Poulenc sent to the Library of Congress to satisfy terms of the Coolidge commission. This manuscript is neatly written and generally free from errors, and it contains considerable revisions when compared to Sources 1 and 3. Absolutely no markings appear on the manuscript which would indicate that it was ever used for performance, but it does contain some tiny notations in black pencil which are similar to those added by engravers as they plan the layout of each page during the process of engraving. Who made these markings and what they mean remains a mystery, but it can be stated unequivocally that this manuscript was not used in the engraving process. Moreover, the lack of performance markings is significant because it helps confirm that other manuscript scores existed which are now missing.

Source 4, in the hand of Poulenc's professional copyist (Monsieur Gunst?)[14], was copied sometime later in 1957 and given by Poulenc to Gareth Morris in preparation for their BBC performance on 16 January 1958. Morris has recalled that Poulenc did not send him a piano score so that he had little conception of the Sonata at the time of first rehearsal with Poulenc. This, the earliest part containing metronome markings, is inscribed 'THE FLUTE PART HAS BEEN REVISED BY JEAN–PIERRE RAMPAL.' We know that this part was lent by Morris to Chester Music and that it was the principal source for the printed flute part (but probably not for the flute part printed in the piano score, which contains significant variants in phrasing).[15]

The preparation of the printed first edition (Source $5a^{s\&p}$) is the subject of considerable uncertainty. Although it was pointed out above that Source 4 was used to produce the printed flute part, Rampal has stated *emphatically* that he did *not* revise the flute part, as is indicated on the part. The statement was probably added by the copyist at Poulenc's direction as a gesture to Rampal for his collaboration during the genesis of the work.[16] Rampal has also stated that he had no contact with Chester concerning the part and noted the irony that his name was misspelled on the first edition.[17]

Precisely how the score was prepared is a complicated web to untangle. Three letters to R. Douglas Gibson from Poulenc mention his plans to transport a manuscript to London. In the first, received at Chester on 29 July 1957, Poulenc advised: 'I will bring you the score of my Sonata on the way to Edinburgh on 2 September.' In a second dated 23 August [1957], Poulenc wrote: 'I will bring to your establishment a *very clean* copy of the Sonata so that engraving it will not be difficult. Concerning the contract, nothing is pressing. I remind you that for this work I require the total sum of 250£.' Finally, in a third letter received by Chester on 30 August 1957, Poulenc wrote 'I will come by Chester Tuesday morning 3 September and bring you the manuscript of my Sonata for Flute.' Whatever manuscript Poulenc finally delivered to Chester has disappeared without a trace.'[18] Apparently the formal contract for the Sonata was signed later when Poulenc delivered his Elegy for Horn and Piano to Chester.[19] Many Poulenc manuscripts used as engraver's copies remain in the hands of his publishers, but in the last half decade of his life he habitually asked for their return, often presenting

---

[13] See Rampal, *Music, My Love,* pp. 125–28 for his account.

[14] Gunst is one of the few copyists employed by Poulenc whose name we know from Poulenc's correspondence.

[15] Many of these variants are catalogued in the two articles by Patricia Harper mentioned in footnote 1.

[16] Poulenc's Sonata for Violin and Piano states 'Partie de violon doigtée et annotée par Ginette NEVEU' and his Sonata for Violoncello and Piano states 'La partie de Violoncelle a été établie par l'auteur en collaboration avec PIERRE FOURNIER.'

[17] Various conversations between Harper and Rampal.

[18] This manuscript is not presently in the collections of either Hansen or Chester and has not been located elsewhere.

[19] Letter to Gibson dated 27 Nov. [1957].

them to special friends or retaining them in his own personal collection.[20]

The next mention of the Sonata in Poulenc's correspondence occurs in a letter from Rome written on 27 January 1958. With it Poulenc returned the set of proofs saying: 'Here, *finally,* are the corrected proofs for the Sonata. One must make a second set that you will have *corrected very carefully* by a *specialist* in order to save time.' Poulenc then requested that a copy of the flute part be sent to him immediately suggesting that Gibson ask Gareth Morris for his part. Poulenc, who needed the part for a performance on the 12th [of February?], added that he would play the piano part from the first proofs if they could be returned to him after corrections had been made. The winter 1958 issue of *The Chesterian* advertised the Sonata as 'in the press' and that it would be 'ready Jan./Feb. 1958.'[21] By June the Sonata still had not been published, and Poulenc expressed his impatience to Gibson on 13 June: 'In effect, my dear Gibson, I do not understand at all the delay with the Sonata. I hope that we will have it soon because people are asking for it everywhere, month after month, all the more so because Rampal is going to promenade it around the world.'

Again we are frustrated by the fact that neither the first nor the second set of corrected proofs can be located and all that remains is a single uncorrected set for the flute part (Source **7b**). Poulenc is known to have worked directly on printed copies in making significant revisions to a few pieces and somewhat more frequently when revising old ones for new editions. Unfortunately, few proofsheets corrected by Poulenc have come to light, and it is suspected that the vast majority of them were simply discarded once the corrections were entered.[22] All that is known to remain of the entire printing process before the edition was published are the Gareth Morris part (Source **4**), several pages of Poulenc's corrections (Source **7a**), of a distinctly minor nature, and the uncorrected proofsheets for the flute part (Source **7b**).

PROBLEMS OF AUTHORITY

In preparing the new edition of the Sonata for Flute and Piano, no single source could be used without careful consideration of the others. There are major differences between the presentation score (Source **2**) and the first printed edition (Source **5a**$^{s\&p}$). Some changes have also been introduced in later 'editions' (reprints) of the printed score and part (Source **5b**$^{s\&p}$). Moreover, the printed score and part contain many inconsistencies in phrasing and various errors of rhythm, pitch, articulation, dynamics, rehearsal numbers, etc. Source **2** has been used as the principal source, but given the fact that neither the manuscript sent to the engraver nor the corrected proofsheets can be located, various emendations have been made on the authority of the printed edition, especially when they are corroborated by Source **8a** (Poulenc's 1957 recording with Rampal), Source **8b** (Poulenc's 1958 recording with Morris), or Source **8c** (Poulenc's 1959 recording with Rampal). All such emendations have been logged in the critical report, and the source of the emendation and the reason for its acceptance discussed. Other variants are logged only if they have significance. In particular, where the old printed edition (Sources **5a**$^{s\&p}$ **& 5b**$^{s\&p}$) is at substantive variance with the new edition, the alternate reading in Sources **5a**$^{s\&p}$ **& 5b**$^{s\&p}$ has been logged.

EDITORIAL CONVENTIONS

The following editorial conventions are observed. Emendations not found in the principal source (Source **2**) are placed in square brackets except for slurs, which contain a strike through the middle. Where Poulenc has provided alternate endings, written-out trills, or cancelled measures, these alternatives are noted, and some are printed as musical examples in the commentary. Measure numbers in italics are added to facilitate the reporting of variants; the rehearsal numbers are Poulenc's own. In reporting, the designation '4.3' indicates measure four, sign three. (Any note, tied note, or rest is considered to be a sign.) The designation '4.3/4 indicates measure four, between signs three and four. The following abbreviations occur: Fl (flute), Pn (piano), rh (right hand), and lh (left hand). All source numbers are printed in bold type. Pitches are noted according to the following system: CC C c c^1 [middle] c^2 c^3 c^4. Notational inconsistencies (directions of stemming and beaming, etc.) are normalized without comment.

---

[20] The *Elégie pour cor et piano,* for example was sold by Poulenc to the Library of Congress, 'Une Chanson de porcelaine', Improvisations 13–15, and *Laudes de Saint Antoine de Padoue* were presented to Madame Lambiotte, the *Elégie (en accords alternés) pour deux pianos* was presented to Christ Schung, *La Courte Paille* was given to Denise Duval, and the Sonatas for Oboe and Clarinet remained in Poulenc's own possession.

[21] See 32, no. 193 (winter 1958): inside rear cover.

[22] On rare occasions he presented proofsheets to such friends as Georges Auric and Nadia Boulanger, but several of Poulenc's publishers made a point of discarding the corrected proofs he returned, and Poulenc would have had to make a special effort to save them from the dustbin.

SELECTED CRITICAL NOTES
Movement 1

Location	*Source and Comment*
Rubric	Reading in **5a**^{s&p} & **5b**^{s&p} emended to follow **2**. **1** & **3** give 'Allegretto manincolico'; **4** gives 'Allegro manlincolico'; **5a**^{s&p} give 'Allegro malincolico' with metronome marking of ♩ = 84, but in **5b**^{s&p} the erroneous 'Allegro malinconico' has returned; **6** gives 'Allegro malincolico'. The editors are aware that Poulenc seems to have accepted the use of 'Allegro' for this movement (see **7a** where 'Allegro malincolico' appears in Poulenc's hand), but feel that his metronome marking is much closer to 'Allegretto' than to 'Allegro'. If anything, his recordings lie under the indicated tempo, not over.
Metronome	Metronome markings appear only in **4**, **5a**^{s&p}, & **5b**^{s&p}. Rampal says that all such markings were added by Poulenc. In the new edition, they have been added in brackets without comment.
Fl: 0.2	**4**, **5a**^{s&p}, & **5b**^{s&p} give '*p*'
Pn: 1.1	**5a**^s & **5b**^s give '*p dolce*'
Fl: 2.4–3.4	**1** & **3** write out the trills as follows:

Ex. 1

Fl: 8.4	'*mf*' added on authority of **1**, **4**, **5a**^{s&p}, & **5b**^{s&p}
Pn: 9.1	**5a**^s & **5b**^s give '*fp*'
Fl: 10.4–11.4	**1** & **3** write out the trills (see Fl: 2.4–3.4 above)
Fl: 11.1 & 11.4	**5a**^s & **5b**^s give tenutos instead of staccatos; **5a**^p & **5b**^p give one staccato and one tenuto
Pn: 18.1–4 (rh)	added on authority of **1** (cf. 116)
Fl: 20.3	**2** gives a quaver rest
Fl: 20.4–21.4	**1** & **3** write out the trills (see Fl: 2.4–3.4)
Fl: 21.1 & 21.4	**5a**^s & **5b**^s lack staccatos (**4**, **5a**^p, & **5b**^p give staccato only for 21.1)
Fl: 25.1/2	**5a**^s & **5b**^s break the phrase here (**8a** does, **8b** does not)
Fl: 27.1/2	**5a**^s & **5b**^s break the phrase here (**8a** does, **8b** does not)
Fl: 29.1/2	**5a**^s & **5b**^s break the phrase here
Fl: 33.1	**5a**^s & **5b**^s give an accent
Pn: 34.1	'sans pédale' added on authority of **5a**^s, **5b**^s, **8a**, **8b**, & **8c**
Fl: 34.2 & 5	**5a**^p & **5b**^p give tenutos
Fl: 35.5	**5a**^s & **5b**^s give an accent; **5a**^p & **5b**^p do not
Fl: 36.1–4	**5a**^p & **5b**^p slur these four notes

Fl: 36.6	**5a**^p & **5b**^p give a tenuto
Fl: 36.11	**3**, **4**, **5a**^p, & **5b**^p give a staccato
Fl: 39.1–3	**5a** & **5b** lack staccatos
Fl: 39.4	**5a**^p & **5b**^p lack a staccato
Fl: 40.2–3	**2** gives staccatos while **1** & **3** give no articulation marks; slurs given on authority of **4**, **5a**^s, **5b**^s, **8a**, **8b**, & **8c**
Fl: 40.4	**2** gives a quaver rest
Fl: 40.6	'*mf*' added on authority of **1**, **5a**^s, & **5b**^s (cf. Pn: 41.1)
Pn: 46.2–48.3 (rh)	**2** lacks slur; added on authority of **5a**^s & **5b**^s (cf. Fl: 42.2–44.2)
Fl: 50.2–4	**4**, **5a**^s, & **5b**^s give the rhythm f² quaver-quaver rest
Fl: 53.1/2	**5a**^s & **5b**^s break the phrase here
Fl: 54.4–55.4	**1** & **3** write out the trills as follows:

Ex. 2

[music example]

Pn: 56.5 (rh)	stem up on c² added on authority of **1** (but given as c¹) and cf. 102.5 (rh)
Fl: 56.7	**5a**^s & **5b**^s give b² natural
Fl: 57.1/2	**5a**^s & **5b**^s break the phrase here
Fl: 60.4	'*f*' added on authority of **4**, **5a**^s, & **5b**^s (cf. Pn: 61)
Fl & Pn: 61.1	'surtout sans ralentir' added on authority of **4**, **5a**^s, & **5b**^s
Pn: 61.5–62.1 (rh)	**5a**^s & **5b**^s contain a slur in the melody
Fl: 62.1–63.1	**5a**^p & **5b**^p lack the tie
Pn: 62.5	**5a**^s & **5b**^s give an accent
Pn: 63.1–5	**5a**^s & **5b**^s give a slur
Fl: 65.1	**4**, **5a**^{s&p}, & **5b**^{s&p} give '*pp*'
Fl: 73.1	**4**, **5a**^{s&p}, & **5b**^{s&p} give 'Un peu plus vite'
Fl: 73.1	**4**, **5a**^{s&p}, & **5b**^{s&p} give '*mf*'
Fl: 73.1–75.10	The phrasing of this passage raises many questions. **1**, **2**, **3**, **5a**^s, & **5b**^s give three phrases as printed. **4**, **5a**^p, & **5b**^p give 6 phrases (73.1–5; 73.6–74.7; 74.8–75.1; 75.2–75.4; 75.5–7; 75.8–10). **8a** & **8c** give one phrase (73.1–75.10). **8b** gives two phrases (73.1–74.7; 74.8–75.10). Cf. the Pn: 80.1–83.2, which also makes three phrases.
Fl: 73.5	dot wanting
Fl: 74.1–2	**5a**^p & **5b**^p lack a tie
Fl & Pn: 76.1	**4**, **5a**^s, & **5b**^s give '*f*'
Fl & Pn: 78.1	**4**, **5a**^{s&p}, & **5b**^{s&p} give '*mf*'
Pn: 79.1–2 (rh)	**5a**^s & **5b**^s give a tenuto over each beat and slur the two chords
Fl: 83.1	**4**, **5a**^s, & **5b**^s give '*mf*'
Pn: 84.1–2 (rh)	**5a**^s & **5b**^s give a crescendo to '*f*'
Pn: 84 beat 2	**5a**^s & **5b**^s lack a tenuto on both chords
Pn: 85.1–3 (rh top)	**5a**^s & **5b**^s lack a tenuto over each chord
Pn: 85.3 (lh)	**5a**^s & **5b**^s give a crotchet
Pn: 86.1	**5a**^s & **5b**^s give '*sf*'
Fl & Pn: 90.1	**2** gives no dynamic change; emended on authority of **4**, **5a**^{s&p}, **5b**^{s&p}, **8a**, & **8b**

| Pn: 90.1–91.1 (rh) | **5a**^s **& 5b**^s lack a tenuto on each chord |
| | |

Pn: 90.1–91.1 (rh)   **5a**ˢ **& 5b**ˢ lack a tenuto on each chord

Fl: 92.1   **4, 5a**ˢ&ᵖ**, & 5b**ˢ&ᵖ give '*f*'

Pn: 92.1   **5a**ˢ **& 5b**ˢ give '*mf*'

Pn: 92.2 (rh)   **5a**ˢ **& 5b**ˢ give a crescendo

Fl: 93.8/9   **2**, as well as **1, 5a**ˢ&ᵖ**, & 5b**ˢ&ᵖ, lack a semiquaver rest; added to **4** in a different hand (Morris's?)

Pn: 93/94   **5a**ˢ **& 5b**ˢ give '*mf*'

Pn: 94.2 (rh)   **5a**ˢ **& 5b**ˢ give a crescendo

Fl: 96.1   **5a**ᵖ **& 5b**ᵖ give '*f*'; **4** gives '*mp*'

Pn: 96.1   **5a**ˢ **& 5b**ˢ give '*mf*'

Fl: 97.2–4   **5a**ˢ **& 5b**ˢ lack the slur

Fl: 98.1–100.2   **5a**ˢ **& 5b**ˢ phrasing differs

Pn: 98.1 (rh)   **5a**ˢ **& 5b**ˢ give a tenuto

Fl: 98.2–4   **5a**ˢ **& 5b**ˢ lack the slur

Pn: 98.4 (lh)   **2** lacks a fermata; added on authority of **5a**ˢ **& 5b**ˢ

Fl: 100.4–101.4   **1 & 3** write out the trills (see Fl: 54.4–55.4 above)

Fl: 101.4   **4, 5a**ᵖ**, & 5b**ᵖ lack a staccato

Pn: 106.1–5 (rh)   **5a**ˢ **& 5b**ˢ give the slur between the notes stems down

Fl: 108.4–109.4   **1 & 3** write out the trills (see Fl: 2.4–3.4 above, but now one octave lower)

Fl: 110.4–10   **4** lacks a crescendo

Pn: 110.5   stem up on g¹ added on authority of **1** (but given as G) and cf. 12.5 (rh)

Fl: 113.2–114.2   **4, 5a**ˢ&ᵖ**, 5b**ˢ&ᵖ**, & 8a** stop the longer phrase and phrase these notes together; **1, 3, & 8b** follow **2** as printed

Pn: 115.1–116.5 (rh)   **5a**ˢ **& 5b**ˢ give a slur

Pn: 115.5–6 & 7–8   slurs added on authority of 17

Pn: 117–121   in **8a, 8b, & 8c** Poulenc clearly stresses the melody

Pn: 118.3 (lh)   **5a**ˢ **& 5b**ˢ lack lower octave

Pn: 119.1–3 (lh)   **2** gives three crotchets; emended on authority of **5a**ˢ**, 5b**ˢ**, & 8a**

Pn: 120.1–121.2   **5a**ˢ **& 5b**ˢ lack lower octaves

Pn: 120.6–8 & 9–12   slurs added on authority of **5a**ˢ **& 5b**ˢ

Fl: 122.1   **2, 5a**ᵖ**, & 5b**ᵖ continue '*mf*' dynamic (which is restated in **3**); **5a**ˢ **& 5b**ˢ give '*p*'

Pn: 122.1–2 (lh)   **5a**ˢ **& 5b**ˢ lack lower octave

Pn: 122.7 & 11 (lh)   **2** gives f¹ sharp; emended on authority of **1, 5a**ˢ**, & 5b**ˢ

Pn: 124.1–2 (lh)   **5a**ˢ **& 5b**ˢ lack lower octave

Fl: 126.1   '*f*' added on authority of **4, 5a**ˢ&ᵖ**, & 5b**ˢ&ᵖ (cf. Pn: 126)

Pn: 126.1 (lh)   **5a**ˢ **& 5b**ˢ give B instead of BB

Fl: 126.1–128.2   **8b** plays this in one phrase

Fl: 127.5   'sans rigueur' added on authority of **4, 5a**ˢ&ᵖ**, 5b**ˢ&ᵖ**, & 7a**

Fl: 127.5–8   **5a**ˢ&ᵖ **& 5b**ˢ&ᵖ give a slur on these notes only

Pn: 127.3 (lh)   'sans rigueur' added on authority of **7a** (cf. Fl in **4**)

Pn: 128.1–4 (rh)   slur added on authority of **5a**ˢ **& 5b**ˢ

Pn: 128.1 & 2 (lh)   **5a**ˢ **& 5b**ˢ lack lower octaves

Pn: 128.4 (rh)   d¹ sharp not tied over in **5a**ˢ **& 5b**ˢ (but tied over in **1**)

Fl: 129.4   [6] added on authority of 130

Pn: 130.1 (lh)   **5a**ˢ **& 5b**ˢ lack lower octave

Fl & Pn: 132 beats 2 & 3   **2** gives a minum followed by an additional measure which has been scratched out; **1** contains a slightly different but similar reading redundant '*p*' omitted

Pn: 133.1   'céder' added on authority of **4, 5a**ˢ&ᵖ**, & 5b**ˢ&ᵖ '*pp*' added on authority of **3**

Fl: 134.3   'céder' added on authority of **4, 5a**ˢ**, & 5b**ˢ

Pn: 134.4 (lh)

Fl: 134–36   **3** contains three different endings and **2** contains a variant of the third ending. Poulenc's decision to change Fl: 134.6 to a g² natural must have been a later decision. The ending in **2** has been emended on authority of **4, 5a**ˢ&ᵖ**, 5b**ˢ&ᵖ**, 8a, & 8b**. The four variant endings include:

Ex. 3

Fl: 136.1   **5a**ˢ **& 5b**ˢ give a crotchet

Movement 2

Location	Source and Comment
Rubric	**1** gives 'Assez ~~Bien~~ Lent'
Pn: 1.1 (lh)	**5a**ˢ **& 5b**ˢ give 'Doucement baigné de pédale'
Fl: 3.1	**5a**ˢ **& 5b**ˢ give a staccato; **5a**ᵖ **& 5b**ᵖ give no articulation
Pn: 3.1–8.4	**5a**ˢ **& 5b**ˢ place slurs over each group of 4 quavers
Fl: 6.2–4	**5a**ᵖ **& 5b**ᵖ lack the slur
Fl: 10.1–2	**2 & 8b** lack a decrescendo; emended on authority of **5a**ˢ&ᵖ**, 5b**ˢ&ᵖ**, & 8a**
Pn: 10.2–8	**2** lacks a decrescendo; emended on authority of **1, 5a**ˢ**, 5b**ˢ**, 8a, 8b, & 8c**
Pn: 13.1 (lh)	**2** omits dot on minim
Pn: 17.1	**5a**ˢ **& 5b**ˢ lack '*p*'
Pn: 17	**5a**ˢ **& 5b**ˢ garble the meaning of the lines indicating the melodic line c²–d²–e² [dot missing] – a¹

Pn: 18.1 (rh)	**5a**ˢ **& 5b**ˢ lack the indication for the thumb and erroneously make the d¹–f¹ a crotchet
Fl: 19.2–5	**4, 5a**ˢ&ᵖ, **& 5b**ˢ&ᵖ give a decrescendo, but it is not played in **8a, 8b, & 8c**
Pn: 22.1–4 & 5–6	**5a**ˢ **& 5b**ˢ lack slurs
Fl & Pn: 23.1	**4, 5a**ˢ&ᵖ, **& 5b**ˢ&ᵖ give '*p*'
Pn: 23.1–2 (lh)	**5a**ˢ **& 5b**ˢ lack lower octaves
Pn: 24.1–2	**5a**ˢ **& 5b**ˢ place the line between a and e flat
Pn: 25.1–2 (lh)	**5a**ˢ **& 5b**ˢ lack lower octaves
Fl: 26.1	**5a**ˢ **& 5b**ˢ erroneously give a quaver rest
Pn: 26.1	**5a**ˢ **& 5b**ˢ give '*mf*'
Fl: 27.1–2	**4, 5a**ˢ&ᵖ, **& 5b**ˢ&ᵖ give a decrescendo
Pn: 28.1 (lh)	**2** erroneously gives a crotchet rest
Fl: 29.1	**5a**ˢ **& 5b**ˢ erroneously give a quaver rest
Fl: 29.8–30.1	**2, 4, 5a**ˢ&ᵖ, **& 5b**ˢ&ᵖ slur only the last two demisemiquavers in 29; emended on authority of **3** (cf. 26.12–27.1)
Fl: 30.1	**5a**ˢ&ᵖ **& 5b**ˢ&ᵖ give a decrescendo, but it is not played in **8a, 8b, & 8c**
Pn 30.1–2 (lh)	**5a**ˢ **& 5b**ˢ lack lower octave
Pn: 30.1–4 (rh)	**5a**ˢ **& 5b**ˢ give a decrescendo
Fl: 33.3	**5a**ˢ **& 5b**ˢ give an f² flat
Fl & Pn: 34	**2** gives a 3/4 bar emended on authority of **4** (Fl), **5a**ˢ&ᵖ, **5b**ˢ&ᵖ, **8a, 8b, & 8c**

Ex. 4

Fl: 35.1	**5a**ˢ **& 5b**ˢ give a decrescendo
Fl: 35.1	**2, 4, 5a**ˢ&ᵖ, **& 5b**ˢ&ᵖ give an accent over the c¹; emended on authority of **1, 3, 8a, & 8b**
Fl: 35.1	**2, 4, 5a**ˢ&ᵖ **& 5b**ˢ&ᵖ give '*f*'; emended on authority of **3** (**1** gives '*pp*')
Pn: 36.1–2, 3–4, 7–8 (lh)	**5a**ˢ **& 5b**ˢ lack slurs
Pn: 39.1	**5a**ˢ **& 5b**ˢ give '*mp*'
Fl: 41.6–8	**4 & 5a**ˢ&ᵖ lack the f² sharp–g²–f² sharp figure which has been added in **5b**ˢ&ᵖ. Rampal (interview) indicated that this is one of the specific changes that Poulenc approved; emended on authority of **5b**ˢ&ᵖ and Rampal; wanting on **8a, 8b, & 8c**
Fl & Pn: 41	**4, 5a**ˢ&ᵖ **& 5b**ˢ&ᵖ give 'en animant' and **8a** hastens the tempo here; emended on these bases

Pn: 41.1–42.6 (lh)	**5a**ˢ **& 5b**ˢ lack staccatos
Pn: 41.3	**5a**ˢ lacks the sharp; emended on authority of **5b**ˢ and context of the measure
Pn: 45	**5a**ˢ **& 5b**ˢ give

Ex. 5

Fl: 47.1–2	tie added on authority of **3, 4, 5a**ˢ&ᵖ, **5b**ˢ&ᵖ, **8a, 8b, & 8c**
Pn: 48.1	**5a**ˢ **& 5b**ˢ give 'céder'
Pn: 50.1 (lh)	**5a**ˢ **& 5b**ˢ lack a tie on the E flat
Pn: 51 beats 1 & 3 (lh)	**5a**ˢ **& 5b**ˢ lack a sostenuto on the C sharp but give one on the C; sostenutos added to both for consistency
Fl: 52.1	'*f*' added on authority of **4, 5a**ˢ&ᵖ, **& 5b**ˢ&ᵖ
Pn: 52.5–6 (lh)	slur added on authority of **5a**ˢ **& 5b**ˢ
Fl: 54	decrescendo added on authority of **1, 3, 5a**ˢ, **& 5b**ˢ (not in **4**)
Pn: 54.2–55.1	in **1** Poulenc gives the fingering 1, 5, 4, 1, 5 (tied over), 1 for the moving line in the lh
Pn: 55.3–8 (lh)	**5a**ˢ **& 5b**ˢ lack slur
Pn: 55.5–6 (rh)	decrescendo added on authority of **5a**ˢ, **5b**ˢ, **8a, 8b, & 8c**
Fl: 56.1	**4, 5a**ˢ&ᵖ, **& 5b**ˢ&ᵖ give '*pp*'
Fl: 57.5–8	**2** gives quaver rest–d² quaver–e² flat quaver; emended to follow **1, 3, 4, 5a**ˢ&ᵖ, **5b**ˢ&ᵖ, **8a, 8b, & 8c** (cf. **4**)
Fl: 60.1	**4, 5a**ˢ&ᵖ, **& 5b**ˢ&ᵖ give '*ppp*'
Pn: 60.1–2 (lh)	**5a**ˢ **& 5b**ˢ lack lower octave
Fl: 62.1	**2** lacks dot on f¹; **1, 4, 5a**ˢ&ᵖ, **& 5b**ˢ&ᵖ give an accent
Pn: 62.1	**5a**ˢ **& 5b**ˢ give '*p*'
Pn: 62.2 (lh)	**5a**ˢ **& 5b**ˢ lack '(dessus)'
Pn: 63.3 (lh)	**5a**ˢ **& 5b**ˢ lack comma
Pn: 64.1 (rh)	**5a**ˢ **& 5b**ˢ lack the fermata

Movement 3

Note: discrepencies in articulations between **5a**ˢ **& 5b**ˢ and the new edition are too numerous to log in this movement. They have been completely logged through 27 after which only the most important cases are mentioned.

Location	*Source and Comment*
Rubric	**2, 4, 5a**ˢ&ᵖ, **& 5b**ˢ&ᵖ all lack rehearsal number 1; emended on authority of **1 & 3**
Pn: 1.1–3 (lh)	**5a**ˢ **& 5b**ˢ lack accent and two staccatos (cf. 20)
Pn: 2.2 (rh)	**1, 2, 5a**ˢ, **& 5b**ˢ give a staccato. The staccato is also given in Pn: 4.2 (rh). **1, 2, & 3**, the three sources in Poulenc's hand, are quite inconsistent in using the staccato mark. Because Poulenc is very consistent in playing it in **8a, 8b, & 8c**, the staccato has been

added in square brackets (but not reported) in both the rh and lh when this figure occurs.

Pn: 4.2 (rh)	**5a^s & 5b^s** lack staccato
Pn: 4.2 (lh)	**5a^s & 5b^s** lack indication of pedal release
Fl: 4.3	**4, 5a^{s&p}, 5b^{s&p}** give '*f*'
Pn: 5.1 & 7.1 (lh)	**5a^s & 5b^s** lack sostenuto marks on f¹ sharp and a¹
Pn: 5.1 (lh)	**5a^s & 5b^s** lack staccato on bottom note
Pn: 6.1 & 8.1 (rh)	**5a^s & 5b^s** give accents
Pn: 6.1–11.2	each note marked staccato; **5a^s & 5b^s** give '*stacc.*'
Fl: 9.3–4, 7–8, & 10.3–4	**1, 2, & 3** give staccatos; emended to slurs on authority of **4, 5a^{s&p}, 5b^{s&p}, 8a, 8b, & 8c**
Pn: 10.2	**1 & 2** give a¹; emended on authority of **5a^s, 5b^s, & 8a**
Fl: 11.1–8	**8a & 8c** slur this in two groups, while **8b** follows what is printed; cf. 202 where **8a, 8b, & 8c** all follow what is printed
Pn: 11.3–12.1	staccatos added on authority of **8a**
Pn: 12 (rh)	**1 & 2** give e¹; quaver followed by quaver and crotchet rests; emended on authority of **5a^s, 5b^s, & 8a**
Pn: 13.1 (rh)	**5a^s & 5b^s** lack sostenuto marks after g¹ sharp and b¹
Pn: 15.4 (rh)	**5a^s & 5b^s** lack accent
Fl: 16.3	**4, 5a^{s&p} & 5b^{s&p}** lack staccatos
Pn: 16.4	**4, 5a^s, & 5b^s** lack staccatos
Pn: 17.2–18.1 (lh)	**2** gives d¹–e¹; both crotchets a seventh above the bass; emended on authority of **5a^s, 5b^s, & 8a**
Pn: 18.3 (lh)	**5a^s & 5b^s** give d¹ in error (cf. 209.3 (lh)); **1 & 3** also give b
Fl: 19.1	**5a^s & 5b^s** lack accent (but given in **4, 5a^p, & 5b^p**)
Pn: 19.1	**5a^s, 5b^s, 8a, & 8b** give no change of dynamics
Pn: 19.1–4	**5a^s & 5b^s** lack staccatos
Pn: 20.1	cf. **1**
Pn: 20.2–3	**5a^s & 5b^s** lack staccatos (cf. **1**)
Pn: 21.1–2 (lh)	emended on authority of **8a**
Pn: 23.1	**5a^s & 5b^s** lack accent
Fl: 24.1–2, 5–6 & 25.1–2	**5a^{s&p} & 5b^{s&p}** lack staccatos
Pn: 24.1–26.4	**5a^s & 5b^s** lack staccatos
Fl: 28.1 & 30.1	**1 & 2** contain full semibreve rests in both mm.; **3** contains a semiquaver b³ altered in Rampal's hand to b² followed by dotted quaver and crotchet rests for 28.1 and a semibreve rest for 30.1; emended on authority of **4, 5a^{s&p}, 5b^{s&p}, 8a, 8b, & 8c**
Fl: 31.3	staccato added to parallel 16.3
Pn: 31.4 (rh)	**2** gives staccato; emended on authority of **5a^s & 5b^s**
Fl: 33.3	note stem and flag wanting
Fl: 39.1–42.1	**2, 4, 5a^{s&p}, & 5b^{s&p}** give two phrases 39.1–40.1 & 40.2–42.1; emended on

	authority of **1, 3, 8a, & 8c** (cf. Pn: 42.1–47.1; see also 63.1–68.4)
Pn: 39.1 (rh)	**2** gives an accent here and in the parallel passage in 62.1; not found in any other source. It is not consistent with the way he plays the passage and has been suppressed in both instances.
Pn: 45.1–48.1 (rh)	continuing slur omitted; emended on authority of 39–41
Fl: 45.3–4	**2** omits the slur; emended on authority of **1, 3, 4, 5a^{s&p}, 5b^{s&p}, 8a, 8b, & 8c**
Pn: 52.1–54.3	**2**, although it has a variant reading of the actual notes, marks this entire passage staccato; on **8a, 8b, & 8c** Poulenc plays staccato
Pn: 55.1 (rh)	**5a & 5b** erroneously give a quaver
Pn: 57.3 (lh)	**1 & 2** give A flat; emended on authority of **5a^s, 5b^s, 8a, 8b, & 8c**
Pn: 59.1 & 61.1 (lh)	d¹ flat and f¹ lack sostenuto marks
Pn: 60.1 (rh)	**5a^s & 5b^s** give an accent which is not played on **8a, 8b, & 8c**
Pn: 62.3–4 (lh)	**1 & 2** repeat the first beat e¹ flat – g¹; emended on authority of **5a^s & 5b^s** (cf. 38). Poulenc probably originally conceived this phrase as parallel to 59–60.
Fl: 63.1–66.1	**2, 4, 5a^{s&p}, & 5b^{s&p}** give two phrases 66.1–67.1 & 67.2–69.1; emended on authority of **1, 3, 8a, 8b, & 8c** (cf. Pn: 66.1–69.1; see also Pn: 42.1–47.1)
Fl & Pn: 63.1	**5a^{s&p} & 5b^{s&p}** give '*mf*'
Pn: 63.1 (rh)	**2** gives an accent here and in the parallel passage in 39.1 not found in any other source. It is not consistent with the way he plays the passage and has been suppressed in both instances.
Pn: 63.1	**4, 5a^s, & 5b^s** lack an accent
Pn: 69.1–70.3	in **8a, 8b, & 8c** Poulenc plays this passage staccato; cf. also 51.1–52.4
Pn: 71.1–82.2	**5a^s & 5b^s** give only the rubrics 'sec.' and 'sans péd.' The individual staccato marks in **1 & 2** have been restored. In 83–86 no staccato marks are given in **1 & 2**. They have been added on the basis of **8a, 8b, & 8c**.
Fl: 73.1	**1, 2, & 3** give semiquaver g² followed by dotted quaver and quaver rests; emended on authority of **4, 5a^{s&p}, & 5b^{s&p}** and on the basis that Poulenc probably altered this figure when he noted that it was not in conformance with similar figures in 74.2–75.1 and 80.2–81.1.
Fl: 74.2–75.1	**1 & 2** give this passage an octave higher; emended on authority of **4, 5a^{s&p}, 5b^{s&p}, 8a, 8b, & 8c**. The flute is silent in **3**.
Pn: 83.1–86.4 (lh)	**1 & 2** lack staccatos
Fl: 85.1–86.1	**2, 5a^{s&p}, & 5b^{s&p}** lack tie; added on authority of 189–90
Fl: 85–86	**4, 5a^{s&p}, & 5b^{s&p}** give a crescendo

Fl: 86.2–87.2   **5a**ᵖ & **5b**ᵖ lack the slur

Pn: 86.4   **5a**ˢ & **5b**ˢ give a g, but **1** & **8a, 8b,** & **8c** confirm the reading in **2**

Pn: 87.1 (rh)   **5a**ˢ & **5b**ˢ give f sharp and d¹, but **1** confirms **2**

Pn:87.1–92.1   **5a**ˢ & **5b**ˢ give only the rubric 'stacc.'

Fl: 92   **2** gives only a d³ sharp quaver followed by quaver and crotchet rests; emended on authority of **3, 4, 5a**ˢ&ᵖ, **5b**ˢ&ᵖ, **8a, 8b,** & **8c**

Fl: 92.1   **5a**ˢ & **5b**ˢ lack accent

Fl: 93.1   **2** lacks dynamic mark; emended on authority of **1, 3, 4, 5a**ˢ&ᵖ, **5b**ˢ&ᵖ and Pn part

Pn: 93.1–4 (rh)   **1** & **2** give d¹–b¹–g¹–b¹; emended on authority of **5a**ˢ, **5b**ˢ, & **8a**

Pn: 95.1–96.1 (rh)   **1** & **2** give d¹–b¹–g¹–b¹–c¹; emended on authority of **5a**ˢ, **5b**ˢ, & **8a**

Pn: 97.1–4 (rh)   **1** & **2** give e¹ flat-c²–a¹ flat-c²; emended on authority of **5a**ˢ, **5b**ˢ, & **8a**

Fl: 98.1–99.1   In **2** Poulenc neglected to indicate the octave transposition as he moved to the second brace.

Fl: 100   **2** lacks dynamic mark; emended on authority of **1, 2, 5a**ˢ, & **5b**ˢ

Pn: 100   **5a**ˢ & **5b**ˢ give '*f*'

Pn: 100.1–103.3   in **8a, 8b,** & **8c** Poulenc plays this passage quasi staccato

Fl: 103.1–2   **2** lacks tie; emended on authority of **4, 5a**ˢ, & **5b**ˢ

Pn & Fl: 104.1   **5a**ˢ & **5b**ˢ marked 'léger et mordant'; **1, 3, 4, 5a**ᵖ, & **5b**ᵖ not marked

Pn: 104.1–111.4   **5a**ˢ & **5b**ˢ lack staccato marks; **1** marked 'staccatissimo'

Fl: 106.1   **2** & **3** give a tenuto; emended on authority of **1, 4, 5a**ˢ&ᵖ, **5b**ˢ&ᵖ, **8a,** & **8b**

Pn: 106.1 & 3   dynamics added on authority of **5a**ˢ, **5b**ˢ, & **8a**

Fl: 106.2 & 107.3   **1, 2,** & **3** give g³; emended on authority of **4, 5a**ˢ&ᵖ, **5b**ˢ&ᵖ, **8a, 8b,** & **8c**

Pn: 106 2   **5a** erroneously gives a c² sharp which is corrected in **5b**ˢ

Pn: 107.1, 109.1, & 111.1 (lh)   **5a**ˢ & **5b**ˢ give accents

Pn: 111.2 (lh)   **1** & **2** give BB & B

Pn: 114.3–4 (rh)   **5a**ˢ & **5b**ˢ lack a decrescendo

Pn: 115.1   **5a**ˢ & **5b**ˢ lack '*mf*'

Fl: 115 (end)   **4, 5a**ˢ&ᵖ, & **5b**ˢ&ᵖ give '*céder*'

Fl & Pn: 117–18   **1, 2,** & **3** give Ex. 6; emended on authority of **4, 5a**ˢ, **5b**ˢ, **8a, 8b,** & **8c**

Ex. 6

Pn: 118   pedal release not in **2, 5a**ˢ, & **5b**ˢ; emended on authority of **1**

Pn: 119.1   **5a**ˢ & **5b**ˢ lack rubric; also in **1**

Pn: 127.1   **5a**ˢ & **5b**ˢ give a decrescendo

Pn: 128.1   **5a**ˢ & **5b**ˢ give '*f*'

Pn: 129.1 (lh)   **2** lacks crotchet rest

Fl: 133.1–3   **1, 2,** & **3** lack a tenuto over each note; emended on authority of **4, 5a**ˢ&ᵖ, **5b**ˢ&ᵖ, **8a,** & **8b** (cf. Pn: 119)

Fl: 134.1   accent found only in **2, 5a**ᵖ, & **5b**ᵖ (cf. Pn: 132)

Pn: 135.1   **5a**ˢ & **5b**ˢ give '*mf*'

Fl: 143.1   **4, 5a**ˢ&ᵖ, & **5b**ˢ&ᵖ give '*mf*'

Fl: 143.3 & 144.3   **4, 5a**ˢ&ᵖ, & **5b**ˢ&ᵖ lack staccatos

Fl: 145.1–147.1   **2** fails to maintain an 8° sign, and the part is notated an octave too low

Fl: 146.1   **5a**ˢ & **5b**ˢ lack accent (also in **4, 5a**ᵖ, & **5b**ᵖ and cf. comment for Fl: 134.1 above)

Fl: 149.1   **4, 5a**ˢ, & **5b**ˢ give '*p*'; **8b** also uses '*p*'

Pn: 149.1   **5a**ˢ & **5b**ˢ give '*stacc.*'

Fl: 149.5–150.1 & Fl: 153.5–156.1   **1–3** give a crotchet d² followed by quaver & semiquaver rests; emended on authority of **4, 5a**ˢ&ᵖ, **5b**ˢ&ᵖ, **8a, 8b,** & **8c**

Pn: 150.2   in 106 Poulenc marks this passage '*f*' & '*p*'; at 151.2 on **8a** & **8c** he makes a noticeable accent, but on **8b** he does not. In **1** & **2** the B minor chord is one octave lower; emended on authority of **5a**ˢ, **5b**ˢ, **8a, 8b,** & **8c**

Pn: 151.1   **5a**ˢ & **5b**ˢ give an accent

Fl: 153.1   **4, 5a**ˢ&ᵖ & **5b**ˢ&ᵖ give '*mf*'

Fl: 158.1–4   **1, 2,** & **3** give c²–e² flat-a² flat-e² flat; emended on authority of **4, 5a**ˢ&ᵖ, **5b**ˢ&ᵖ, **8a, 8b,** & **8c**

Fl: 160.1–4   **1, 2,** & **3** give e² flat-g² flat-c³ flat-g² flat; emended on authority of **4, 5a**ˢ&ᵖ, **5b**ˢ&ᵖ, **8a, 8b,** & **8c**

Pn: 161.1   pedal indication added on authority of **5a**ˢ, **5b**ˢ, **8a, 8b,** & **8c**

Fl: 161.2–165.2   **2** lacks all ties; emended on authority of **4, 5a**ˢ&ᵖ, **5b**ˢ&ᵖ, **8a, 8b,** & **8c**

Pn: 164.2   **5a**ˢ & **5b**ˢ lack the lower octave c², which also occurs in **1**

Fl & Pn: 167   **1** & **2** give 'Subito le double plus lent', **3** gives 'Double plus lent', & **4, 5a**ˢ&ᵖ, & **5b**ˢ&ᵖ give 'Subito più lento ♩ = 66'. Rampal has said that 'Subito deux fois plus lent' would be more correct French. See Harper's letter to the editor in *The Flutist Quarterly* 17, No. 3 (1992): 7. The metronome marking is actually less than half the tempo.

Fl: 167.1   **4, 5a**ˢ&ᵖ, & **5b**ˢ&ᵖ give '*f*'

Fl: 167.1–168.5   **8b** gives two phrases; **8a** & **8c** give two phrases: 167.1–4 and 167.5–168.5

Pn: 169.1 | **5a^s & 5b^s** give no dynamic & place an accent on beat one (rh)

Fl: 170.1 | **4, 5a^{s&p}, & 5b^{s&p}** give '*p*'

Pn: 173.1–2 (rh) | **2** gives c^1-b natural

Fl: 174.1 | **4, 5a^{s&p}, & 5b^{s&p}** give no new dynamic; **1 & 3** confirm '*f*'; **8a & 8c** play '*p*' and **8b** '*pp*'

Pn: 175.1–186.4 | cf. 71.1–82.4, the parallel passage, in which Poulenc marks the lh staccato

Fl: 183.1–4 & 187.1–4 | **1, 2, & 3** slur the semiquavers in groups of four; emended on authority of **4, 5a^{s&p}, 5b^{s&p}, 8a, 8b, & 8c**, which slur the semiquavers in pairs

Fl: 189.1 | '*ff*' added on authority of **4, 5a^{s&p}, 5b^{s&p}, 8a, 8b, & 8c** (cf. Pn)

Fl: 189–190 | **2** lacks ties

Pn: 189.1–190.1 | **5a^s & 5b^s** lack accents on lower part of rh

Fl & Pn: 190/191 | **1 & 2** give an extra m. identical to 189 at this point; emended on authority of **4, 5a^p, 5b^p, 8a, 8b, & 8c**

Fl: 191.2–192.1 | **5a^s & 5b^s** lack slur, which is also found in **1, 4, 5a^p, & 5b^p**

Pn: 191.3 (rh) | **1, 2, & 8a** give e instead of the f given in **5a^s & 5b^s**

Fl: 192.1 | **2, 5a^{s&p}, & 5b^{s&p}** give a redundant '*ff*'

Fl & Pn: 192–210 | In essence this passage mirrors 1–19. The reading in **2** is not consistent with its earlier statement in **2** or with those in **5a^{s&p} & 5b^{s&p}**. Source **2** clearly replaces some staccato marks with tenutos, which have not been retained in the edition. Moreover, the articulation in the flute part in 200–201 differs from that in 9–11 & 24–25.

Pn: 193.3–94 (lh) | '*sans pédale*' added (cf. 2.3-3.1 (lh))

Pn: 195.1–2 (lh) | '*[Péd. *]*' added (cf. 4.1–2 (lh))

Pn: 197.1 (rh) | **5a^s & 5b^s** give both an accent and a tenuto (cf. 6)

Fl: 197.5 | staccato added to parallel 6.5 (also in **1 & 3**)

Fl: 198.4 | staccato added to parallel 6.5 (also in **1 & 3**)

Pn: 199.1 (rh) | **5a^s & 5b^s** give both an accent and a tenuto (cf. 8)

Pn: 200.1–203.1 | **2** lacks staccatos; emended to parallel 9.1–12.1

Pn: 201.2 | **1 & 2** give a^1; emended on authority of **5a^s, 5b^s, & 8a**

Pn: 203.1 | **1 & 2** give e^1 quaver followed by quaver and crotchet rests; emended on authority of **5a^s, 5b^s, & 8a** (cf. 12)

Pn: 205.1 (rh) | **5a^s & 5b^s** lack accent

Pn: 206.2–3 (rh) | **5a^s & 5b^s** lack a slur

Fl: 207.3 | staccato added to agree with 16.3 and 31.3

Pn: 207.4 | **5a^s & 5b^s** give no change in dynamics

Pn: 208.2 (lh) | **2** gives d^1–e^1 both crotchets a seventh above the bass; emended on authority of **5a^s, 5b^s, & 8a** (cf. 17)

Pn: 210.1 | **5a^s & 5b^s** give an a^1 above the f^1 sharp

Pn: 210.3 | **2** gives e–d^1–g^1 sharp-c^2 sharp; emended on authority of **8a**

Fl: 211 | **4, 5a^{s&p}, & 5b^{s&p}** give a crotchet and crotchet rest (cf. 20)

Fl: 215 | **1 & 2** give crotchet e^3 plus quaver and crotchet rests; emended on authority of **5a^{s&p}, 5b^{s&p}, 8a, & 8b**

Fl: 217.1 | **4, 5a^{s&p}, & 5b^{s&p}** give '*mf*'

Pn: 218.1 (rh) | **5a^s & 5b^s** lack d^2 flat & tenuto

Pn: 218.1–4 (lh) | **2** adds four quavers e flat-b-flat, d^1 flat-f^1 over the e flat minim

Pn: 219.1 | **5a^s & 5b^s** give '*f*' (which is consistent with the Pn part)

Pn: 220.1 | **2** gives this an octave lower; emended on authority of **8a**

Pn: 222.1 | **5a^s & 5b^s** lack a tenuto

Pn: 232.3 (rh & lh) | **5a^s & 5b^s** give accents

Fl: 233.3–236.1 | **2** lacks a slur; emended on authority of **4, 5a^{s&p}, 5b^{s&p}, 8a, 8b, & 8c**

Acknowledgments

The editors are most grateful to the following individuals for their assistance and courtesies: Jean-Pierre Rampal, for granting interviews and for making available Source **3**; Gareth Morris, for granting an interview and for making available Sources **4** and **8b**; and Julius Baker, for granting several interviews. In addition they thank James Pruett, Head of the Music Division, Library of Congress, for permission to quote from Music Division Old Correspondence, the letters of Francis Poulenc, and Source **2**; J. Rigbie Turner, Mary Flagler Cary Curator of Music Manuscripts and Books at the Pierpont Morgan Library, for permission to consult Source **1**; James Rushton, for permission to quote from Poulenc's letters in the possession of Chester Music; and Rosine Seringe, owner of the *droits morales* of Francis Poulenc.

Carl B. Schmidt, Editor
Patricia Harper, Consulting Editor

INTRODUCTION HISTORIQUE[1]

La première allusion faite par Francis Poulenc à une sonate pour flûte qu'il était en train d'écrire apparaît dans une lettre à son ami le baryton Pierre Bernac datée du 2 septembre (1952). Il y confiait: "Momentanément j'ai délaissé la Sonate pour deux pianos pour la Sonate de flûte qui a tout à coup pris corps à la Gare d'Austerlitz jeudi dernier."[2] La nouvelle fut confirmée par la livraison d'octobre du *The Chesterian*, revue officielle de Chester Music, dans laquelle on lisait: "Francis Poulenc écrit en ce moment une Sonate pour flûte et piano dont on espère qu'elle pourra être publiée au début de l'année prochaine. Cette oeuvre est composée expressément à l'intention d'une flûtiste américain célèbre qui la créera aux Etats-Unis"[3], le "flûtiste américain célèbre" étant très probablement Julius Baker, alors sur le point de quitter sa situation de soliste du Chicago Symphony pour retourner à New York et occuper les fonctions de professeur à la Juilliard School et de membre de l'Orchestre de CBS et du Bach Aria Group[4]. Trois lettres de Poulenc adressées à son éditeur R. Douglas Gibson, chez Chester, attestent du fait que le musicien projeta la composition de l'oeuvre pendant plusieurs années. Il écrivit en 1953: "Je termine actuellement ma Sonate pour deux pianos. Dieu sait si je reprendrai jamais celle de flûte car je vais écrire un grand opéra pour La Scala d'après les *Dialogues des Carmélites*."[5] Il ajouta en 1955: "Après l'été, j'espère reprendre mon idée de Sonate de flûte" et, enfin, remarqua début 1956: "Peut-être cet été je finirai la Flute Sonata."

On ignore si cette sonate "précoce" correspond directement à celle qui fut éditée mais cela paraît vraisemblable. Dans une lettre datée du 3 avril 1956, Harold Spivacke, directeur du département de la musique de la Bibliothèque du Congrès (Washington), agissant en tant que porte-parole de la Fondation Coolidge de la Bibliothèque du Congrès, écrivit à Poulenc pour lui proposer la commande d'une pièce de musique de chambre destinée à un festival qui devait avoir lieu du 19 au 21 octobre 1956[6]. Bien qu'évoquant une pièce pour deux pianos, Spivacke laissait à Poulenc la liberté de choisir un autre type d'oeuvre dans la mesure où elle n'excéderait pas une formation de six instruments. Poulenc déclina la commande

dans une lettre du 13 avril [1956], expliquant qu'il était en train de terminer l'orchestration de son opéra dont la création à Milan était imminente. Nullement découragé, Spivacke renouvela son offre dans une lettre datée du 9 mai 1956. Poulenc retarda sa réponse jusqu'au mois d'août et indiqua à ce moment-là que, son opéra étant achevé, il pouvait désormais envisager d'écrire une pièce. Il soumit le projet d'une sonate pour flûte et piano dédiée à la mémoire d'Elizabeth Sprague Coolidge et accepta les principes d'une rémunération de $750 et du don du manuscrit original à la Bibliothèque du Congrès à la condition de pouvoir réserver la création de l'oeuvre au festival de Strasbourg en juin 1957.

Jean-Pierre Rampal prit connaissance du projet de la sonate par un appel téléphonique de Poulenc, peu après la commande. Dans son autobiographie, Rampal en rappelle les circonstances: "Jean-Pierre, dit Poulenc, vous avez toujours désiré que j'écrive une sonate pour flûte et piano? Et bien, je vais le faire et le meilleur c'est que les Américains vont me payer pour cela! J'ai reçu une commande de la Fondation Coolidge pour écrire une pièce de musique de chambre à la mémoire d'Elizabeth Coolidge. Je ne l'ai jamais connue, j'estime donc que la pièce vous appartient."[7]

D'autres lettres échangées entre Poulenc et Spivacke ou ses assistants conclurent l'accord et Poulenc écrivit l'oeuvre à Cannes entre décembre 1956 et mars 1957. Dans une lettre à Bernac datée du 8 mars [1957], Poulenc qualifia la Sonate d'oeuvre de proportions "debussystes". Le 9 mars 1957, Poulenc tint R. Douglas Gibson au courant de l'avancement de son travail: "Les deux premiers mouvements de la Sonate sont faits. J'en suis content. Il s'agit d'un *allegro melancolico* et d'une *cantilena*. Le Final sera un *allegro giocoso*." Il dut achever le *finale* rapidement car dès le 7 juin 1957, onze jours avant sa création de l'oeuvre avec Rampal au festival de Strasbourg, il en expédia le manuscrit complet à la Bibliothèque du Congrès[8]. Poulenc avait à l'origine l'intention de se rendre aux Etats-Unis pour apporter l'oeuvre à la Bibliothèque du Congrès et proposa même d'y donner un récital avec la chanteuse Alice Esty qui aurait compris la

---

[1] La documentation exposée dans cette introduction est empruntée à Carl B. Schmidt, *A Catalogue of the Music of Francis Poulenc (1899–1963)*, Oxford (Grande-Bretagne), (Oxford University Press, à paraître) et aux articles de Patricia Harper "A Fresh Look at Francis Poulenc's *Sonata for Flute and Piano*", dans *The Flutist Quarterly* 17, No. 1 (1992), pp. 8–23 et "A Further Look at Francis Poulenc's *Sonata for Flute and Piano*", dans *The Flutist Quarterly* 18, No. 2 (1993/94), pp. 48–57. Voir aussi sa lettre à la rédaction dans *The Flutist Quarterly* 17, No. 3 (1992), p. 7.

[2] Voir la correspondance non publiée à Paris, Bibliothèque nationale, Département des manuscrits.

[3] Voir vol. 27, No. 172 (oct. 1952), p. 40.

[4] Entretiens privés entre P. Harper et J. Baker (25 août et 16 octobre 1993).

[5] Voir les lettres non publiées de Poulenc des 23 avril (1953), 17 juin [1955] et 25 février [1957], Londres, Archives J. W. Chester.

[6] Pour la correspondance entre Poulenc, Spivacke et ses assistants, voir "Music Division Old Correspondence" à la Library of Congress, Washington D.C.

[7] Jean-Pierre Rampal, *Music, My Love: An Autobiography with Deborah Wise* (New York, Random House, 1989), pp. 125–6. Pour un récit similaire mais un peu différent, voir Katherine Goll-Wilson, "Jean-Pierre Rampal on Making Music", *Flute Talk* 10 (Mai 1991), pp. 9–13.

[8] La première audition non officielle, donnée le 17 juin 1957, est rapportée ainsi par Rampal: "La veille de la représentation, Poulenc m'appela dans la matinée. "Arthur Rubinstein est ici" dit-il. "Je viens de lui parler et il aimerait beaucoup entendre ma nouvelle sonate. Le seul problème c'est qu'il doit partir demain avant le concert. Pourriez-vous venir maintenant pour une répétition supplémentaire?" "Avec plaisir" lui répondis-je. C'est ainsi que la création officieuse . . . eut lieu dans une salle de concert de Strasbourg devant un public d'une personne — Arthur Rubinstein, assis au milieu de premier rang. Les applaudissements qu'il nous réserva sont restés gravés dans ma mémoire à l'égal de ceux reçus après les autres concerts que j'ai donnés". Voir Rampal, *Music, My Love*, p. 128.

deuxième audition américaine de son cycle de mélodies *Le Travail du peintre*[9]. Cependant, réalisant que ce concert constituerait l'unique raison de son déplacement, il changea d'idée et suggéra que la création américaine de la Sonate soit assurée par Rampal et son pianiste Robert Veyron-Lacroix. La création américaine qui eut lieu au Coolidge Auditorium de la Bibliothèque du Congrès le 14 février 1958 remporta, selon les critiques des journaux et une lettre de Spivacke à Poulenc, un succès éclatant[10].

Entre sa création mondiale et sa création américaine, Poulenc trouva le temps de présenter la sonate au monde anglophone par l'intermédiaire de la BBC, canal qu'il avait utilisé à plusieurs reprises depuis les années 1920. Le 16 janvier 1958, Poulenc y joua l'oeuvre avec le célèbre flûtiste anglais Gareth Morris[11]. Dès ces premières exécutions, et Poulenc allait en donner d'autres avant sa mort, la Sonate pour flûte et piano devint l'une des sonates pour flûte les plus régulièrement jouées et les plus appréciées de tout le répertoire[12]. Par cette nouvelle édition, les éditeurs espèrent non seulement clarifier de nombreuses ambiguïtés textuelles mais également fournir une documentation suffisante sur les origines de l'oeuvre et les principales difficultés impliquées par son édition.

LES SOURCES

Les sources suivantes, désignées par leurs sigles numériques, ont servi à l'établissement de cette nouvelle édition.

1. Brouillon de partition autographe (Etats-Unis, New York City, Pierpont Morgan Library, Frederich R. Koch Foundation 639). Ce manuscrit fut offert par Poulenc à son médecin personnel et porte l'inscription de la main de Poulenc: "Pour mon ange / gardien, le cher / Docteur Chevalier / tendrement / Poulenc / [régle]." Il est daté "Majestic / Cannes / Décembre / 56" après le premier mouvement et "Majestic / Cannes / Décembre [1956] / Mars / 37" après le troisième mouvement. Cette source fait pendant à la source **3**.

2. Partition autographe en donation (Etats-Unis, Washington D.C., Library of Congress, ML29c.P78 no. 1 case). Adressée par Poulenc le 7 juin 1957 en accord avec les termes de la commande de la Fondation Coolidge.

3. Partie séparée de flûte autographe (France, collection personnelle de Jean-Pierre Rampal). Utilisée en vue de la création, le 17 juin 1957, cette source fait pendant à la source **1**.

4. Partie séparée de flûte copiée (Grande-Bretagne, collection personnelle de Gareth Morris). Utilisée pour la première exécution en Angleterre diffusée par la BBC et dédicacée à Morris par Poulenc le 16 janvier 1958. Ce manuscrit porte les inscriptions "Pour Monsieur Morris / qui joue si merveilleusement / cette Sonate / avec un bien amical / merci. / Fr. Poulenc / [règle] / 16/1/58" et "Day of the first *Carmélites* / performance" [Jour de la première des *Carmélites*], toutes deux de la main de Poulenc.

5a. Premières partition (**5a**[s]) et partie séparée (**5a**[p]) imprimées (Londres, J. & W. Chester Ltd. (J. W. C. 1605)), © 1958 "Printed in Denmark" et "WILHELM HANSENS NODESTIK OG TRYK KØBENHAVN. 1958 PRINTED IN DENMARK"; 23p. + [i] ; 30cm et partie séparée 8p.; portant la mention "The flute part has been revised by JEAN-PIERRE RAMPEL [sic]". Egalement appelée "16ème édition", la plus courante actuellement, cette édition ne comporte que d'infimes variantes par rapport à la première et ne représente pas une nouvelle édition au sens technique. Il s'agit, en fait, d'un retirage photographique contenant quelques modifications mineures.

5b. Editions 2–16 publiées par Chester: partition (**5b**[s]) et partie séparée (**5b**[p]). Voir description ci-dessus.

6. Pulenk, F. Sonata dlya flcity i f-p. (Red. partii fleity Zh. Rampel'). M.:Muzgiz, 1966. [Poulenc, F. Sonate pour flûte et pianoforte. [Edition de la partie de flûte J. Rampel [Jean-Pierre Rampal]]. Edition de V. Zverev, Moscou, Muzgiz, 1966]. 24p. (partition), 8p. (partie séparée); 29cm; 3240 exemplaires; 39 kopecks. Cette édition, établie d'après l'édition **5a**[s&p] n'a pas été collationnée. (Un exemplaire en est conservé à la Bibliothèque du Congrès).

7a. Deux pages de corrections de détail de la main de Poulenc qu'il envoya à J. W. Chester avant la publication imprimée de la partition et de la partie séparée (Grande-Bretagne, Londres, archives J. W. Chester).

7b. Un jeu d'épreuves non corrigées de la partie de flûte (Grande-Bretagne, Londres, archives J. W. Chester).

---

[9] Voir la lettre de Poulenc datée du 7 juin [1957].

[10] Voir la critique de Day Thorpe dans *The Evening Star* (Washington D.C.), 19 février 1958 et la lettre de Spivacke datée du 24 février 1958 dans laquelle il écrit : "Je vous écris pour vous dire que l'exécution par MM. Rampal et Veyron-La Croix de votre Sonate pour flûte et piano a remporté un grand succès. La réaction du public a été des plus enthousiastes et je tiens à vous faire savoir qu'à la Music Division nous l'avons immensément appréciée." Un enregistrement de cette exécution fut envoyé à Poulenc et une copie conservée à la Bibliothèque du Congrès.

[11] Une bande d'enregistrement de cette exécution, dont la BBC s'est défaite et qui est maintenant en la possession de M. Morris, a été consultée pour établir cette édition.

[12] Pour une liste détaillée d'enregistrements, y compris ceux de Poulenc, voir Francine Bloch, *Phonographies Francis Poulenc 1928–1982* (Paris, Bibliothèque Nationale, 1984), pp. 186–190. Voir en particulier les deux enregistrements réalisés avec Rampal en 1957 et 1959 et un troisième réalisé avec Christian Lardé au Festival de Menton le 3 juillet 1962. Dans une lettre à Gibson, datée du 14 novembre [1957], Poulenc écrit du premier: "Je suis heureux de vous annoncer que l'enregistrement de la Sonate pour flûte [et piano] est excellent."

8a. Enregistrement sonore réalisé par Jean-Pierre Rampal et Francis Poulenc au moment de la première exécution publique de Strasbourg (18 juin 1957).

8b. Enregistrement sonore réalisé par Gareth Morris et Francis Poulenc pour une émission de la BBC, 16 janvier 1958. (Copie en possession de Morris.)

8c. Enregistrement sonore réalisé par Jean-Pierre Rampal et Francis Poulenc en juin 1959 dans le cadre de la série "Présence de la musique contemporaine" (Véga C 35 A 181; nouvelle gravure par Wergo référence WER 50004, ca 1963). L'ingénieur du son était Pierre Rosenwald.

Rapport entre les sources existantes et les Sources Manquantes

Dans son autobiographie, Jean-Pierre Rampal raconte que Poulenc, alors en pleines répétitions de la production parisienne de *Dialogues des Carmélites* (créé le 18 juin 1957), le convoqua à plusieurs reprises dans son appartement du 5 rue de Médicis pour jouer la sonate au fur et à mesure de son élaboration[13]. Rampal explique qu'à première vue: "le premier mouvement semblait décousu et il ne s'en dégageait pas vraiment un thème ou une direction. Les idées allaient et venaient sans réelle cohérence et certains doigtés étaient impossibles. Je le lui dis." A une autre occasion, Rampal rapporte: "Je vis que ses idées s'avéraient plus cohérentes cette fois mais étaient encore loin d'être accomplies." A la fin de ces séances, Poulenc confiait aparemment quelques esquisses musicales à Rampal afin de "voir si c'était jouable". Ces rencontres se poursuivirent et Rampal nota: "J'ai changé quelques phrasés ici et là et donné à Francis quelques idées sur la façon dont l'oeuvre devrait s'organiser . . . mais je ne voyais tout simplement pas où cette pièce se dirigeait — et craignais que Francis ne le vît pas non plus. Néanmoins, il prit de l'assurance et, lentement mais sûrement, la Sonate pour flûte et piano atteint sa forme définitive."

Il est regrettable qu'aucun des fragments manuscrits mentionnés ci-dessus par Rampal n'ait survécu. La première trace écrite de la Sonate en est une réduction pour piano rudimentaire sur laquelle Poulenc inscrivit en première page "monstre brouillon" (source **1**). Ce manuscrit donne de nombreuses orientations de composition et représente à l'évidence une des premières étapes de la conception de l'oeuvre. Il comporte plusieurs mesures supprimées par la suite et une formule initiale d'accompagnement du premier mouvement qui devait être considérablement remaniée avant la publication de l'oeuvre.

La partie séparées de flûte transcrite de la main de Poulenc (source **3**), dont Rampal indique qu'elle fut utilisée en vue de la création à Strasbourg, reprend la source **1** sur de nombreux points (nuances dynamiques, transcriptions des trilles, transpositions à l'octave, suppressions de certains passages, localisation de la numérotation de travail, etc.). Il semblerait que Rampal proposa des modifications à cette partie pendant les répétitions avec Poulenc avant la création car ses annotations corrigent souvent des éléments écrits par Poulenc. Cette partie n'est pas celle sur laquelle furent copiées ni la source **4**, ni les partitions imprimées (sources **5a**$^{s\&p}$ et **5b**$^{s\&p}$).

La seule copie exacte du manuscrit de l'oeuvre est la source **2**, exemplaire envoyé par Poulenc à la Bibliothèque du Congrès pour honorer les termes de la commande de la Fondation Coolidge. Celui-ci est écrit avec netteté et, généralement sans erreurs. Il contient des modifications notables par rapport aux sources **1** et **3**. Aucune inscription indiquant qu'il aurait été utilisé pour une quelconque exécution ne figure sur le manuscrit, en revanche de très petites notations au crayon noir, similaires à celles des graveurs disposant chaque page pour la gravure, y sont portées. L'auteur de ces notations et leur signification demeurent énigmatiques. On peut, toutefois, affirmer sans équivoque que ce manuscrit ne fut pas utilisé pour la gravure. De plus, l'absence d'annotations d'exécution est significative en ce qu'elle confirme l'existence d'autres partition manuscrites perdues aujourd'hui.

La source **4**, de la main du copiste professionnel de Poulenc (Monsieur Gunst?)[14], fut copiée plus tard au cours de l'année 1957 et offerte par Poulenc à Gareth Morris en vue de leur exécution pour la BBC du 16 janvier 1958. Morris raconta que Poulenc ne lui avait pas envoyé la partie de piano et qu'il n'avait donc qu'une faible notion de la Sonate lors de sa première répétition avec Poulenc. Cette partie séparée, la première contenant des indications métronomiques, porte l'inscription "THE FLUTE PART HAS BEEN REVISED BY JEAN-PIERRE RAMPAL" [La partie de flûte a été revue par Jean-Pierre Rampal]. On sait que Morris prêta cette partie à Chester Music et que celle-ci constitua la source principale d'après laquelle fut imprimée la partie séparée de flûte (mais sans doute pas la partie de flûte imprimée au-dessus de la partie de piano qui présente des différences marquantes de phrasé)[15].

La préparation du tirage de la première édition (source **5a**$^{s\&p}$) reste entourée d'une grande incertitude. En dépit de l'affirmation précédente de l'utilisation de la source **4** pour le tirage de la partie séparée de flûte, Rampal a déclaré avec insistance qu'il n'avait *pas* revu la partie de flûte contrairement à ce qui est indiqué sur la partition. Cette annotation fut probablement ajoutée par le copiste à la demande de Poulenc en geste de gratitude vers Rampal pour sa collaboration à la genèse de l'oeuvre[16]. Rampal a également précisé qu'il n'eut aucun contact avec Chester au sujet de cette partie et observa que l'ironie voulut que son nom ait été mal orthographié sur la première édition[17].

---

[13] Voir le récit de Rampal dans: *Music. My Love*, pp. 125–128.
[14] Gunst est l'un des quelques copistes employés par Poulenc dont le nom est connu grâce à la correspondance du musicien.
[15] Nombre des variantes sont cataloguées dans les deux articles de Patricia Harper cités dans la note 1.
[16] La Sonate pour violon et piano de Poulenc porte la mention: "Partie de violon doigtée et annotée par Ginette NEVEU" et sa Sonate pour violoncelle et piano: "La partie de violoncelle a été établie par l'auteur en collaboration avec PIERRE FOURNIER."
[17] Entretien entre P. Harper et J. P. Rampal.

La façon dont la partition fut précisément préparée demeure un enchevêtrement difficile à démêler. Trois lettre adressées par Poulenc à R. Douglas Gibson font état de son projet d'apporter un manuscrit à Londres. Dans la première, parvenue chez Chester le 29 juillet 1957, Poulenc affirme: "Je vous porterai la Sonate en allant à Edimburgh le 2 septembre." Dans la deuxième, datée du 23 août [1957], Poulenc écrit: "J'apporterai à votre maison une copie *très nette* de la Sonate ce qui ne rendra pas difficile la gravure. Pour le contrat rien ne presse. Je vous rappelle que je désire pour cette oeuvre la somme nette de 250 livres." Enfin dans la troisième reçue le 30 août 1957, Poulenc précise: "Je passerai (mardi le 3 sept.) au matin chez Chester. Je vous apporterai le manuscrit de ma Sonate de flûte." Le manuscrit que Poulenc confia finalement à Chester a disparu sans laisser de trace[18]. Le contrat formel pour la Sonate fut, semble-t-il, signé plus tard lorsque Poulenc apporta son *Elégie* pour cor et piano chez Chester[19]. De nombreux manuscrits de Poulenc utilisés pour la gravure sont restés entre les mains de ses éditeurs. Toutefois, pendant ses cinq dernières années, il chercha fréquemment à les récupérer pour les offrir à des amis ou les conserver dans sa collection personnelle[20].

L'allusion suivante faite à la Sonate dans la correspondance de Poulenc apparaît dans la lettre écrite de Rome, le 27 janvier 1958, accompagnant les épreuves de la partition: "Voici *enfin* les épreuves corrigées de la Sonate. Qu'on en fasse une seconde épreuve que vous ferez *corriger très soigneusement* par un *spécialiste*. Ceci pour gagner du temps." Poulenc ensuite souhaite qu'on

lui envoie immédiatement un exemplaire de la partie de flûte suggérant à Gibson de demander sa partie séparée à Gareth Morris. Poulenc, qui avait besoin de cette partie pour une exécution le 12 [février?], ajoute qu'il jouerait la partie de piano sur les premières épreuves si l'on pouvait les lui retourner après avoir effectué les corrections. La livraison de l'hiver 1958 de *The Chesterian* annonçait la Sonate "sous presse" et qu'elle serait "prête en janvier/février 1958"[21]. En juin, la Sonate n'était toujours pas publiée et Poulenc exprima son impatience à Gibson le 13 juin: "En effet, mon cher Gibson, je ne comprenais rien au tard de la Sonate. J'espère que nous l'aurons bientôt car on la réclame partout d'autant plus que, pendant des mois et des mois, Rampal va la promener à travers le monde."

On est, une fois de plus, frustré par le fait que ni le premier ni le second jeux d'épreuves ne peuvent être localisés et qu'il ne reste qu'un seul jeu non corrigé de la partie de flûte (source **7b**). On sait que Poulenc s'est directement servi des tirages imprimés de quelques-unes de ses pièces pour y effectuer des rectifications importantes et, plus fréquemment, pour réviser d'anciennes oeuvres en vue de leur réédition. Malheureusement, on dispose de peu de pages corrigées par Poulenc et on peut supposer que, dans la vaste majorité des cas, elles ont été tout simplement détruites une fois les corrections faites[22]. Les seuls témoignages de la procédure d'impression précédant la publication de la sonate sont la partie séparée de Gareth Morris (source **4**), plusieurs feuillets de corrections de détail de Poulenc (source **7a**) et le jeu d'épreuves non corrigé de la partie de flûte (source **7b**).

QUESTIONS D'AUTORITE

On ne pouvait, pour l'établissement de cette nouvelle édition de la Sonate pour flûte, considérer une seule source sans envisager soigneusement les autres. Il existe des différences majeures entre la partition en donation (source **2**) et la première édition imprimée (source **5a**^**s&p**). Quelques changements sont également intervenus dans des "éditions" (retirages) ultérieures de la partition complète et de la la partie séparée (source **5b**^**s&p**). De plus la partition et la partie séparée imprimées comportent de nombreuses incohérences quant au phrasé et diverses erreurs de rythme, de hauteurs, d'articulation, de nuances, de numérotation de travail, etc. La source **2** a été utilisée comme source principale, mais, en l'absence du manuscrit

envoyé au graveur et des épreuves corrigées lors de la première édition, plusieurs modifications ont été introduites sur l'autorité de la source imprimée, surtout lorsqu'elles sont corroborées par la source **8a** (enregistrement de Poulenc et Rampal de 1957), la source **8b** (enregistrement de Poulenc et Morris de 1958) ou la source **8c** (enregistrement de Poulenc et Rampal de 1959). Toutes ces modifications sont signalées dans les notes critiques ainsi que leur origine et leur motif. Quelques autres variantes ne sont relevées que si elles présentent une signification certaine. En particulier, la version alternative des sources **5a**^**s&p** et **5b**^**s&p** est notée lorsque celle-ci montre un écart important avec la nouvelle édition.

[18] Ce manuscrit ne se trouve ni dans les archives de Hansen, ni dans celles de Chester et n'a pas été localisé ailleurs.

[19] Lettre à Gibson datée du 27 novembre [1957].

[20] L'*Elégie pour cor et piano*, par exemple, fut vendue par Poulenc à la Bibliothèque du Congrès, "Une chanson de porcelaine", Improvisations 13–15 et *Laudes de Saint Antoine de Padoue* furent offerts à Madame Lambiotte, l'*Elégie (en accords alternés) pour deux pianos* fut offerte à Christ Schung, *La Courte Paille* fut donnée à Denise Duval et les Sonates pour hautbois et clarinette demeurèrent en la possession de Poulenc.

[21] Voir 32, No. 193 (hiver 1958), troisième de couverture.

[22] A de rares occasions, il offrit des jeux d'épreuves à des amis, ainsi Georges Auric et Nadia Boulanger. Plusieurs des éditeurs de Poulenc insistaient pour faire disparaitre les épreuves corrigées qu'il leur renvoyait et Poulenc dut déployer des efforts spéciaux pour les sauver de la corbeille à papiers.

CONVENTIONS EDITORIALES

Les conventions éditoriales suivantes ont été respectées. Les remaniements qui ne figurent pas dans la source principale (source **2**) sont placés entre parenthèses, à l'exceptions des liaisons de phrasé qui sont barrées en leur milieu. Là où Poulenc avait prévu des terminaisons différentes, la transcription de trilles ou la suppression de mesures, ces versions sont notées et certaines imprimées en exemples musicaux dans le commentaire. Une numérotation en italiques des mesures a été ajoutée pour faciliter le repérage des variantes. La numérotation de travail est de Poulenc. L'indication "4.3" signifie mesure 4, signe 3 (toutes notes, notes liées ou figures de silence sont considérées comme des signes). L'indication "4.3/4" désigne la mesure 4 entre les signes 3 et 4. Les abréviations suivantes ont été utilisées: Fl (flûte), Pn (piano), rh (main droite), lh (main gauche). Les numéros correspondant aux sources sont imprimés en caractères gras. Les hauteurs respectent le système suivant: DoDo Do do do^1 (médium) do^2 do^3 do^4. Les erreurs de notation (direction des hampes et des barres transversales, etc.) ont été rectifiées sans commentaire.

HISTORISCHE EINLEITUNG[1]

Francis Poulenc erwähnte seine Flötensonate erstmals in einem Brief vom 2. September [1952] an seinen Freund, den Bariton Pierre Bernac, in dem er bemerkte, 'Ich habe die Sonate für zwei Klaviere zugunsten einer Flötensonate beiseite gelegt, die im Bahnhof Austerlitz am Donnerstag plötzlich Gestalt annahm.'[2] Die Bestätigung dessen erschien in der Oktoberausgabe des *Chesterian*, der offiziellen Zeitschrift von Chester Music, in der es hieß: 'Francis Poulenc schreibt zur Zeit eine Sonate für Flöte und Klavier, die voraussichtlich zu Beginn des nächsten Jahres veröffentlicht wird. Das Werk ist eine Komposition für einen bekannten amerikanischen Flötisten, der es in den Vereinigten Staaten vorstellen wird.'[3] Dieser 'bekannte amerikanische Flötist' war sehr wahrscheinlich Julius Baker, der zu jener Zeit kurz davor stand, seine Stellung als Leiter des Chicago Symphony Orchestras aufzugeben und nach New York als Lehrer an die Juilliard School zurückzukehren und um mit dem CBS Orchestra und der Bach Aria Group aufzutreten.[4] Drei Briefe Poulencs an seinen Verleger R. Douglas Gibson bei Chester weisen darauf hin, daß sich Poulenc über einige Jahre hinweg mit dem Gedanken trug, das Werk fortzusetzen. 1953 schrieb er: 'Ich stelle gerade meine Sonate für zwei Klaviere fertig. Wer weiß, ob ich jemals wieder zur Flötensonate finde, denn ich werde eine große Oper für La Scala schreiben, die auf den *Dialogues des Carmélites* beruht.'[5] 1955 fügte er hinzu, 'Am Ende des Sommers hoffe ich mich wieder an meine Idee für eine Flötensonate machen zu können.' Anfang 1956 schrieb Poulenc schließlich, 'Diesen Sommer werde ich vielleicht die Flötensonate fertigstellen.'

Es ist nicht bekannt, ob diese 'frühe' Sonate direkt mit der Veröffentlichten verwandt ist, es ist jedoch sehr wahrscheinlich. In einem Brief vom 3. April 1956 schrieb Harold Spivacke, Vorsitzender der Musikabteilung der Library of Congress, in seiner doppelten Eigenschaft als Sprecher der Coolidge Stiftung an der Library of Congress an Poulenc und bot ihm einen Auftrag für ein Kammermusikstück anläßlich eines Festivals an, das vom 19. bis 21. Oktober 1956 stattfinden sollte.[6] Obwohl Spivacke ein Stück für zwei Klaviere vorschlug, ließ er Poulenc die Wahl, auch ein anderes Werk zu komponieren, vorausgesetzt, daß es nicht mehr als sechs Instrumente enthielt.

Poulenc antwortete in seinem Brief vom 13. April [1956] und lehnte den Auftrag ab, da er gerade dabei wäre, die Instrumentierung seiner Oper fertigzustellen und ihre Premiere in Mailand kurz bevorstünde. Spivacke blieb unbeeindruckt und bot ihm den Auftrag erneut in einem Brief vom 9. Mai 1956 an. Poulenc zögerte seine Antwort bis zum August hinaus, als er meinte, daß seine Oper nun in Ordnung war und er gedenke, etwas schreiben zu können. Er schlug eine Sonate für Flöte und Klavier zum Andenken an Elizabeth Sprague Coolidge vor und stimmte Spivackes Honorar von $750 sowie der Vereinbarung zu, daß das Originalmanuskript der Library of Congress zum Geschenk gemacht werde, vorausgesetzt, daß Poulenc mit der Premiere bis zum Straßburger Festival im Juni 1957 warten könne.

Jean-Pierre Rampal hörte offenbar von der Sonate durch einen Anruf Poulencs kurz nach der Auftragserteilung. Rampal erinnert sich in seiner Autobiographie an das Ereignis: 'Jean-Pierre', sagte Poulenc, 'Wolltest Du nicht schon immer, daß ich eine Sonate für Flöte und Klavier schreibe? Genau das werde ich jetzt tun', sagte er. 'Und das Schönste ist, daß die Amerikaner es bezahlen werden! Die Coolidge Stiftung hat mir den Auftrag erteilt, ein Kammermusikstück zum Andenken an Elizabeth Coolidge zu schreiben. Ich kannte sie nicht, das Stück ist meiner Meinung nach deshalb das *Deine*.'[7]

Weitere Briefe zwischen Poulenc und Spivacke und seinen Bevollmächtigten machten die Vereinbarung komplett, und Poulenc schrieb das Werk im französischen Cannes zwischen Dezember 1956 und März 1957. In einem Brief an Bernac vom 8. März [1957] nannte Poulenc die Sonate ein Werk von 'Debussyschen' Verhältnissen. Am 9. März 1957 berichtete Poulenc R. Douglas Gibson von seinem Fortschritt: 'Die ersten beiden Sätze der Sonate sind fertig. Ich bin mit ihnen zufrieden. Es handelt sich um ein *Allegretto melancolico* und eine *Cantilena*. Das Finale wird ein *Allegro giocoso*.' Poulenc hat das Finale wohl sehr schnell beendet, denn am 7. Juni 1957, nur elf Tage bevor er zusammen mit Rampal die Welturaufführung beim Straßburger Festival vorstellte, schickte er das vollständige Manuskript an die Library of Congress.[8] Anfänglich hatte Poulenc die Absicht, nach den Vereinigten Staaten zu reisen, um das

---

[1] Die in dieser Einleitung enthaltene information stammt aus Carl B. Schmidts *A Catalogue of the Music of Francis Poulenc (1899–1963)* (Oxford, England: Oxford University Press, in Vorbereitung) und aus Patricia Harpers Artikel 'A Fresh Look at Francis Poulenc's *Sonata for Flute and Piano*,' *The Flutist Quarterly* 17, No. 1 (1992): 8–23 und 'A Further Look at Francis Poulenc's *Sonata for Flute and Piano*,' *The Flutist Quarterly* 18, No. 2 (1993/94): S. 48–57. Vergleiche auch ihren Brief an den Herausgeber in *The Flutist Quarterly* 17, No. 3 (1992): 7.

[2] Vergleiche den unveröffentlichten Brief in Paris, Bibliothèque Nationale, Manuskriptabteilung. Alle in dieser Ausgabe zitierten Briefe Poulencs wurden von dem Herausgeber aus dem Französischen übertragen.

[3] Vergleiche Vol. 27, No. 172 (Oct. 1952): 40.

[4] Privatgespräche zwischen Harper und Baker (25. August und 16. Oktober 1993).

[5] Vergleiche Poulencs unveröffentlichte Briefe vom 23. April [1953], 17. Juni [1955], und 25. Februar [1957] London, J. W. Chester Archive.

[6] In bezug auf diesen und andere Briefe zwischen Poulenc, Spivacke und Mitarbeitern, vergleiche 'Music Division Old Correspondence' in der Library of Congress in Washington, D.C.

[7] Jean-Pierre Rampal, *Music, My Love: An Autobiography with Deborah Wise* (New York: Random House, 1989), S. 125–6. Für eine ähnliche aber nicht identische Darstellung vergleiche Katherine Goll-Wilson, 'Jean-Pierre Rampal on Making Music,' *Flute Talk* 10 (May 1991): 9–13.

[8] Die inoffizielle Premiere fand am 17. Juni 1957 statt. Mit Rampals Worten: 'Poulenc rief mich am Morgen vor der ersten Aufführung an. "Arthur Rubinstein ist hier," sagte er. "Ich habe gerade mit ihm gesprochen, und er würde sehr gern meine neue Sonate hören. Das Problem ist jedoch, daß er morgen schon vor der Aufführung abfahren muß. Könntest Du vielleicht jetzt

Werk in der Library aufzuführen und schlug sogar ein Konzert mit der Sängerin Alice Esty vor, in dem auch sein Liederkreis *Le Travail du peintre* zum zweiten Mal in Amerika aufgeführt werden sollte[9]. Als er bemerkte, daß dieses Konzert der einzige Grund für seine Amerikareise wäre, zögerte er und schlug vor, daß Rampal und sein Pianist Robert Veyron-Lacroix die amerikanische Uraufführung spielen sollten. Sie fand am 14. Februar 1958 im Coolidge Auditorium der Library of Congress statt und war laut Zeitungsmeldungen und einem Brief von Spivacke an Poulenc ein gewaltiger Erfolg.[10]

Zwischen der Welturaufführung und der amerikanischen Uraufführung hatte Poulenc noch Zeit gefunden, die Sonate der englischsprachigen Welt in der BBC vorzustellen,

ein Forum, das er bei zahlreichen Anlässen seit den 1920er Jahren benutzt hatte. Am 16. Januar 1958 spielte Poulenc das Werk mit dem bekannten englischen Flötisten Gareth Morris.[11] Seit diesen frühen Aufführungen — und Poulenc sollte bis zu seinem Tod noch weitere geben — ist die Sonate für Flöte und Klavier zu einer der am häufigsten gespielten und beliebtesten Flötensonaten im gesamten Repertoire geworden.[12] Die Herausgeber hoffen, mit der vorliegenden Ausgabe nicht nur zahlreiche textliche Fragen zu klären, sondern auch genügend dokumentarische Belege für jene zu liefern, die mehr über den Hintergrund des Werks und die bei seiner Herausgabe wichtigen Probleme erfahren möchten.

DIE QUELLEN

Die folgenden Quellen mit ihren numerischen Sigeln wurden bei der Vorbereitung dieser neuen Ausgabe verwendet.

1. Autographer Partiturentwurf (Vereinigte Staaten: New York City, Pierpont Morgan Library, Frederich R. Koch Foundation 639). Poulenc gab dieses Manuskript seinem Hausarzt und es trägt die Widmung in Poulencs Handschrift 'Pour mon ange / gardien, le cher / Docteur Chevalier / tendrement / Poulenc / [rule].' Das Manuskript ist datiert 'Majestic / Cannes / Décembre / 56' nach dem ersten Satz und 'Majestic / Cannes / Décembre [1956] / Mars 57' nach dem dritten Satz. Gehört zu Quelle 3.

2. Autographe Schenkungspartitur (Vereinigte Staaten: Washington D.C., Library of Congress, ML29c.P78 no. 1 case). Von Poulenc am 7. Juni 1957 geschickt, um den Bedingungen des Auftrags der Coolidge Stiftung nachzukommen.

3. Autographe Flötenstimme (Frankreich: Privatbibliothek von Jean-Pierre Rampal). Wurde bei den Vorbereitungen für die erste Aufführung am 17. Juni 1957 verwendet. Gehört zu Quelle 1.

4. Flötenstimme des Kopisten (Großbritannien: Privatbibliothek von Gareth Morris). Wurde bei der ersten englischen Aufführung durch die BBC verwendet und Morris am 16. Januar 1958 von Poulenc

gewidmet. Dieses Manuskript trägt die Widmung 'Pour Monsieur Morris / qui joue si merveilleusement / cette Sonate / avec un bien amical / merci. / Fr. Poulenc / [rule] / 16/1/58' und 'Day of the first *Carmélites* / performance' (Tag der ersten Aufführung der *Carmélites*), beides in Poulencs Handschrift.

5a. Erste gedruckte Partitur (**5a^s**) und Stimme (**5a^p**) (London: J. & W. Chester, Ltd. (J.W.C. 1605)), © 1958; 'Printed in Denmark' und 'WILHELM HANSENS NODESTIK OG TRYK KØBENHAVN. 1958 PRINTED IN DENMARK'; 23S. + [i]; 30cm und Stimme 8S.; mit Vermerk 'The flute part has been revised by JEAN-PIERRE RAMPEL [sic]' (Die Flötenstimme wurde von JEAN-PIERRE RAMPEL [sic] überarbeitet). Die sogenannte '16th edition', die bis jetzt aktuellste, enthält nur geringe Abweichungen wenn man sie mit der ersten Ausgabe vergleicht, und stellt rein theoretisch keine neue Ausgabe dar. Sie ist vielmehr ein photographischer Nachdruck mit gelegentlichen kleinen Änderungen.

5b. Ausgaben 2–16 von Chester gedruckt: Partitur (**5b^s**) und Stimme (**5b^p**). Für eine Erläuterung siehe oben.

6. Pulenk, F. Sonata dlya fleity i f-p. [Red. partii fleity Zh. Rampel]. M.: Muzgiz, 1966. [Poulenc, F. Sonate für Flöte und Klavier. [Herausgeber der Flötenstimme J. Rampel [Jean-Pierre Rampal]]. Herausgegeben von V. Zverev, Moskau: Muzgiz, 1966]. 24S. (Partitur), 8S.

gerade 'mal vorbeikommen und ein letztes Mal proben?" "Mit Vergnügen," sagte ich. Die inoffizielle Premiere fand somit . . . in einem Straßburger Konzertsaal mit einem Zuhörer statt — Arthur Rubinstein, der mitten in der ersten Reihe saß. Der Applaus, den wir von ihm erhielten, war so bemerkenswert wie bei jedem anderen Konzert, das ich gegeben habe.' Vergleiche Rampal, *Music, My Love*, S. 128.

[9] Vergleiche Poulencs Brief vom 7. Juni [1957].

[10] Vergleiche Day Thorpes Kritik in *The Evening Star* (Washington D.C.), 19 Feb. 1958 und Spivackes Brief vom 24. Feb. 1958, in dem er schrieb: 'Ich schreibe, um Ihnen mitzuteilen, daß die Aufführung Ihrer Sonate für Flöte und Klavier von den Herren Rampal und Veyron-La Croix ein großer Erfolg war. Das Publikum war sehr enthusiastisch, und ich möchte, daß Sie wissen, daß uns das Stück in der Musikabteilung auch sehr gut gefallen hat.' Eine Aufnahme dieser Aufführung wurde an Poulenc geschickt und eine Kopie in der Library of Congress zurückbehalten.

[11] Eine Aufnahme dieser von der BBC ausrangierten und jetzt im Besitz von Herrn Morris befindlichen Aufführung war von den Herausgebern für diese Ausgabe zu Rate gezogen worden.

[12] Für eine ausführliche Liste von Aufnahmen einschließlich jener von Poulenc vergleiche Francine Bloch, *Phonographies Francis Poulenc 1928–1982* (Paris: Bibliothèque Nationale, 1984), S. 186–90. Vergleiche besonders die beiden Aufzeichnungen mit Rampal 1957 und 1959 und eine dritte beim Festival de Menton mit Christian Lardé am 3. Juli 1962. Poulenc schrieb in einem Brief an Gibson vom 14. Nov. [1957] über die erste, 'Ich freue mich, Ihnen sagen zu können, daß die Aufnahme der Sonate für Flöte [und Klavier] ausgezeichnet ist.'

(Stimme); 29cm; 3240 Exemplare; 39 Kopeken. Diese Ausgabe, die auf **5a^{s&p}** (siehe oben) beruht, wurde nicht zusammengestellt. (Kopie in Library of Congress.)

7a. Zwei Seiten mit kleineren Verbesserungen in Poulencs Handschrift, die Poulenc an J. W. Chester schickte ehe die gedruckte Partitur und Stimme veröffentlicht wurden (Großbritannien: London, J. W. Chester-Archiv).

7b. Ein Satz nicht verbesserter Korrekturfahnen für die Flötenstimme (Großbritannien: London, J. W. Chester-Archiv)

8a. Eine Aufnahme von Jean-Pierre Rampal und Francis Poulenc zur Zeit der ersten Aufführung in Straßburg (18. Juni 1957).

8b. Eine Aufnahme von Gareth Morris und Francis Poulenc für eine Übertragung der BBC, 16. Januar 1958. (Kopie im Besitz von Morris)

8c. Eine Aufnahme von Jean-Pierre Rampal und Francis Poulenc im Juni 1959 als Teil der Reihe 'Présence de la Musique Contemporaine' (Véga C 35 A 181; von Wergo als WER 50004 ca. 1963 neu herausgegeben). Der Tontechniker war Pierre Rosenwald.

Verhältnis Quellen und Fehlenden Quellen

Jean-Pierre Rampal berichtet in seiner Autobiographie, daß Poulenc ihn während der Proben für die Pariser Inszenierung der *Dialogues des Carmélites* (erstmals am 18. Juni 1957 aufgeführt) wiederholt in seine Wohnung in die 5 rue de Médicis bestellt habe, um die Sonate während ihres Entstehens durchzuspielen.[13] Rampal meinte nach einem ersten Blick: 'Der erste Satz schien zusammenhanglos, und ein Thema oder eine Richtung waren kaum vorhanden. Die Ideen kamen und gingen, es gab jedoch keinen richtigen Zusammenhalt. Und der Fingersatz war teilweise unmöglich. Ich habe ihm das gesagt.' Beim zweiten Mal berichtet Rampal, 'Ich merkte, daß seine Ideen dieses Mal verständlicher waren, aber noch immer nicht vollendet.' Poulenc schickte ihn anscheinend mit einigen Notenstücken weg, um zu 'sehen, ob sie spielbar sind.' Es gab weitere Treffen, und Rampal schrieb: 'Ich habe hier und da einige Phrasen geändert und Francis einige Vorschläge gemacht, wie das Werk zusammenhängen sollte . . . ich konnte aber einfach nicht erkennen, worauf das Stück hinauslief. — und fürchtete sehr, daß Francis es auch nicht sah. Er wurde dennoch zuversichtlicher, und langsam aber sicher nahm die Sonate für Flöte und Klavier ihre endgültige Gestalt an.'

Leider ist uns keines der von Rampal oben erwähnten Manuskriptfragmente überliefert, und die früheste bekannte Aufzeichnung der Sonate ist die unfertige Klavierpartitur, die Poulenc als 'monstre Brouillon' auf der ersten Seite bezeichnete (Quelle **1**). Dieses Manuskript enthält zahlreiche Kompositionsansätze und stellt eindeutig eine frühe Stufe des Werks in Poulencs Entwurf dar. Es weist verschiedene durchgestrichene Takte auf, und die primäre begleitende Figur im ersten Satz sollte zahlreiche beachtliche Überarbeitungen durchlaufen, ehe das Werk veröffentlicht wurde.

Die Flötenstimme in Poulencs Handschrift (Quelle **3**), die laut Rampal für die Vorbereitung der Straßburger Uraufführung verwendet worden war, folgt Quelle **1** in vielen Einzelheiten (Dynamik, ausgeschriebene Triller, Oktavversetzungen, durchgestrichene Passagen, Stellung der Probenummern usw.). Rampal nahm offenbar an seinem Teil — wahrscheinlich während der Proben mit Poulenc für die Uraufführung — Änderungen vor, da seine Hinzufügungen häufig Einzelheiten revidieren, die

Poulenc geschrieben hatte. Dieser Teil ist nicht jener, von dem entweder Quelle **4** oder die gedruckten Partituren (Quellen **5a^{s&p}** & **5b^{s&p}**) kopiert worden waren.

Die einzige Manuskriptreinschrift des Werks ist Quelle **2**, das Exemplar, das Poulenc an die Library of Congress schickte, um den Bedingungen des Coolidge Auftrags nachzukommen. Dieses Manuskript ist sauber geschrieben und im großen und ganzen fehlerlos. Auch enthält es im Vergleich zu den Quellen **1** und **3** beachtliche Überarbeitungen. In dem Manuskript kommen überhaupt keine Markierungen vor, was darauf hinweist, daß es nie für eine Aufführung verwendet wurde, es enthält jedoch einige kleine Anmerkungen mit Bleistift, die jenen ähneln, die Notenstecher hinzufügen, wenn sie die Anlage einer jeden Seite während des Stechens planen. Es bleibt unklar, wer diese Markierungen machte und was sie bedeuten, es läßt sich jedoch eindeutig festlegen, daß dieses Manuskript nicht für das Stechen verwendet worden war. Auch ist der Mangel an Aufführungsanmerkungen bemerkenswert, da er darauf hinweist, daß andere Manuskriptpartituren vorhanden waren, die mittlerweile verlorengegangen sind.

Quelle **4** in der Handschrift von Poulencs professionellem Kopisten (Monsieur Gunst?)[14], wurde 1957 kopiert und Poulenc gab sie Gareth Morris zur Vorbereitung auf ihre BBC Aufführung am 16. Januar 1958. Morris erinnerte sich, daß Poulenc ihm keine Klavierpartitur geschickt hatte, so daß er zur Zeit der ersten Probe mit Poulenc kaum Vorstellungen von der Sonate hatte. Diese Quelle, deren frühester Teil Metronombezeichnungen enthält, trägt die Inschrift 'THE FLUTE PART HAS BEEN REVISED BY JEAN-PIERRE RAMPAL.' Wir wissen, daß Morris Chester Music diese Stimme geliehen hat und er die Hauptquelle für den gedruckten Flötenteil war (wahrscheinlich jedoch nicht für den Flötenteil, der in der Klavierpartitur abgedruckt ist und bedeutende Abweichungen in der Phrasierung enthält).[15]

Die Vorbereitung der gedruckten ersten Ausgabe (Quelle **5a^{s&p}**) ist Gegenstand beachtlicher Ungewißheit. Obwohl oben gezeigt wurde, daß Quelle **4** für die Herstellung des gedruckten Flötenteils verwendet wurde, hat Rampal *nachdrücklich* darauf hingewiesen, daß er

---

[13] Vergleiche Rampal, *Music, My Love*, S. 125–28 für seinen Bericht.

[14] Gunst ist einer der wenigen Kopisten, die Poulenc beschäftigte und dessen Name uns aus Poulencs Briefwechsel bekannt ist.

[15] Viele dieser Varianten sind in den zwei in Fußnote 1 erwähnten Artikeln von Patricia Harper katalogisiert.

den Flötenteil *nicht* überarbeitet hat, wie es auf der Stimme heißt. Diese Aussage war vermutlich von dem Kopisten auf Anweisung Poulencs hinzugefügt worden, als Geste an Rampal für seine Mithilfe bei der Entstehung des Werks.[16] Rampal hat auch betont, daß er mit Chester bezüglich der Stimme keinen Kontakt hatte, und auf die Ironie hingewiesen, daß sein Name auf der ersten Ausgabe falsch geschrieben worden war.[17]

Genau festzustellen, wie die Partitur vorbereitet wurde, ist ein kompliziertes Unterfangen. Poulenc erwähnt in drei Briefen an R. Douglas Gibson seine Pläne für den Transport eines Manuskripts nach London. Im ersten, der Chester am 29. Juli 1957 erreichte, bemerkte Poulenc: 'Ich werde Ihnen die Partitur meiner Sonate auf meinem Weg nach Edinburgh am 2. September bringen.' In einem zweiten, datiert vom 23. August [1957], schrieb Poulenc: 'Ich werde Ihrer Firma eine *sehr saubere* Kopie der Sonate bringen, so daß das Setzen keine Schwierigkeiten bereiten dürfte. Was den Vertrag betrifft, so besteht keine Eile. Ich erinnere Sie daran, daß ich für dieses Werk den Gesamtbetrag von 250£ benötige.' Und schließlich schrieb Poulenc in einem dritten Brief, der Chester am 30. August 1957 erreichte 'Ich komme Dienstagmorgen, am 3. September, bei Chester vorbei und bringe Ihnen das Manuskript meiner Flötensonate.' Was für ein Manuskript auch immer Poulenc bei Chester ablieferte, es ist spurlos verschwunden.[18] Der formale Vertrag für die Sonate wurde offenbar später unterschrieben, als Poulenc seine Elegie für Horn und Klavier bei Chester ablieferte.[19] Viele Manuskripte Poulencs, die von den Stechern verwendet wurden, blieben in den Händen seiner Verleger; in seinen letzten fünf Lebensjahren bat er jedoch meistens um ihre Rücksendung und gab sie häufig guten Freuden zum Geschenk oder behielt sie in seinem persönlichen Besitz.[20]

Der nächste Hinweis auf die Sonate in Poulencs Briefwechsel findet sich in einem Brief aus Rom vom 27. Januar 1958. Poulenc schickte zusammen mit ihm die Korrekturfahnen zurück und sagte: 'Hiermit erhalten Sie *endlich* die korrigierten Korrekturfahnen der Sonate. Es sollte ein zweiter Satz angefertigt werden, den sie *sehr sorgfältig von einem Spezialisten korrigieren* lassen werden, um Zeit zu sparen.' Poulenc bat ferner darum, daß eine Kopie des Flötenteils sofort an ihn geschickt werde, und schlug vor, daß Gibson Gareth Morris um seinen Teil bat. Poulenc, der diesen Teil für eine Aufführung am 12. [Februar?] benötigte, fügte hinzu, daß er den Klavierteil aus den ersten Korrekturfahnen spielen werde, wenn sie nach Anfertigung der Korrekturen wieder an ihn geschickt werden könnten. Die 1958er Winterausgabe des *Chesterian* kündigte die Sonate als 'in the press' (im Druck befindlich) an und wies darauf hin 'ready Jan./Feb. 1958'.[21] Im Juni war die Sonate immer noch nicht gedruckt, und Poulenc äußerte am 13. Juni seine Ungeduld gegenüber Gibson: 'Mein lieber Gibson, ich verstehe wirklich nicht die Verzögerung bei der Sonata. Ich hoffe, daß wir sie bald erhalten, da die Leute überall nach ihr fragen, Monat um Monat, zumal Rampal sie in der ganzen Welt aufführen wird.'

Es ist wieder frustierend, daß weder der erste noch der zweite Satz der korrigierten Korrekturfahnen auffindbar ist und uns nur ein einzelner unkorrigierter Satz des Flötenteils vorliegt (Quelle **7b**). Poulenc soll bekanntlich direkt mit gedruckten Exemplaren gearbeitet haben und bedeutende Veränderungen an einigen Stücken vorgenommen haben besonders, wenn er alte Exemplare für neue Ausgaben überarbeitete. Leider sind nur wenige Korrekturfahnen, die von Poulenc korrigiert wurden, aufgetaucht, und man vermutet, daß die Mehrzahl einfach vernichtet wurde, nachdem die Korrekturen gemacht worden waren.[22] Alles was bekanntlich von dem gesamten Druckprozess vor Veröffentlichung der Ausgabe übrig geblieben ist, ist der Teil von Gareth Morris (Quelle **4**), zahlreiche Seiten von Poulencs Korrekturen (Quelle **7a**) von eindeutig unwichtigerer Natur und die unkorrigierten Korrekturfahnen des Flötenteils (Quelle **7b**).

PROBLEME MIT DEN QUELLEN

Bei der Vorbereitung der neuen Ausgabe der Sonate für Flöte und Klavier konnte keine einzige Quelle verwendet werden, ohne nicht auch die anderen sorgfältig zu prüfen. Es gibt große Unterschiede zwischen der Schenkungspartitur (Quelle **2**) und der ersten gedruckten Ausgabe (Quelle **5a**$^{s\&p}$). In späteren 'Ausgaben' (Nachdrucken) der gedruckten Partitur und Stimme wurden ebenfalls einige Änderungen vorgenommen (Quelle **5b**$^{s\&p}$). Darüber hinaus enthalten die gedruckte Partitur und Stimme zahlreiche Widersprüche bezüglich der Phrasierung und verschiedene Fehler, was Rhythmus, Tonhöhe, Artikulation, Dynamik, Probenummern usw. betrifft. Quelle **2** wurde als Hauptquelle verwendet; angesichts der Tatsache, daß weder das Manuskript, das an den Setzer geschickt worden war, noch die korrigierten Korrekturfahnen auffindbar sind, wurden zahlreiche Verbesserungen in

[16] In Poulencs Sonate für Violine und Klavier heißt es 'Partie de violon doigtée et annotée par Ginette Neveu' und in seiner Sonate für Violoncello und Klavier 'La partie de Violoncelle a été établie par l'auteur en collaboration avec Pierre Fournier.'

[17] Verschiedene Gespräche zwischen Harper und Rampal.

[18] Dieses Manuskript befindet sich zur Zeit weder in der Sammlung von Hansen noch in der von Chester und konnte auch woanders nicht gefunden werden.

[19] Brief an Gibson datiert 27. Nov. [1957].

[20] Die *Elégie pour cor et piano* wurde zum Beispiel von Poulenc an die Library of Congress verkauft, 'Une Chanson de porcelaine', Improvisations 13–15, und *Laudes de Saint Antoine de Padoue* wurden Madame Lambiotte geschenkt, die *Elégie (en accords alternés) pour deux pianos* war ein Geschenk für Christ Schung, *La Courte Paille* gab Poulenc Denise Duval, und die Sonaten für Oboe und Klarinette blieben in Poulencs Besitz.

[21] Vergleiche 32, No. 193 (Winter 1958): hinterer Innenumschlag.

[22] Gelegentlich schenkte er Freunden wie Georges Auric und Nadia Boulanger Korrekturfahnen; zahlreiche von Poulencs Verlegern bestanden aber darauf, die korrigierten Korrekturfahnen, die er ihnen schickte, zu vernichten, und Poulenc hätte besondere Anstrengungen unternehmen müssen, um sie vor dem Papierkorb zu retten.

bezug auf die Autorität der gedruckten Ausgabe vorgenommen, besonders wenn sie durch Quelle **8a** (Poulencs 1957er Aufnahme mit Rampal), Quelle **8b** (Poulencs 1958er Aufnahme mit Morris) oder Quelle **8c** (Poulencs 1959er Aufnahme mit Rampal) bestätigt wurden. Diese Verbesserungen wurden jedoch alle im kritischen Kommentar vermerkt und die Quelle der Änderungen sowie die Gründe für ihre Annahme diskutiert. Andere Varianten wurden nur vermerkt, wenn sie von Bedeutung waren. Besonders, wo die alte gedruckte Ausgabe (Quellen **5a**$^{s\&p}$ & **5b**$^{s\&p}$) sich beträchtlich von der neuen Ausgabe unterscheidet, wurde die abweichende Lesart in Quellen **5a**$^{s\&p}$ & **5b**$^{s\&p}$ vermerkt.

GEPFLOGENHEITEN DER HERAUSGEBER

Folgende herausgeberische Gepflogenheiten wurden beachtet. Verbesserungen, die in der Hauptquelle (Quelle **2**) nicht vorhanden waren, stehen in eckigen Klammern mit Ausnahme von Schleifern, die einen Strich durch die Mitte erhalten. Wo Poulenc für abweichende Abschlüsse, ausgeschriebene Triller oder durchgestrichene Takte sorgte, werden diese Alternativen vermerkt, und einige erscheinen als musikalische Beispiele im Kommentar. Taktzahlen in Schrägschrift wurden hinzugefügt, um die Angabe von Varianten zu erleichtern; die Probenummern stammen von Poulenc. Im kritischen Kommentar bezeichnet '4.3' Takt vier, Zeichen drei. (Jede Note, gebundene Note oder Pause wird als Zeichen angesehen.) '4.3/4' bedeutet Zählzeit vier, zwischen Zeichen drei und vier. Die folgenden Abkürzungen kommen vor: Fl (Flöte), Pn (Piano), rh (rechte Hand), und lh (linke Hand). Alle Quellennummern erscheinen in Fettdruck. Für Tonhöhen wurde folgendes System verwendet: CC C c c^1 [mittleres] c^2 c^3 c^4. Widersprüche in der Notation (Richtung der Hälse und Balken, usw.) wurden kommentarlos vereinheitlicht.

SONATE
pour
Flûte et Piano

FRANCIS POULENC (1957)

1 Allegretto malincolico

[mettre beaucoup de pédale (les doubles croches très estompées)]

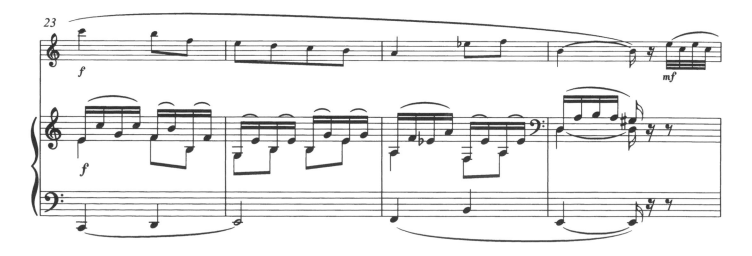

Flute

SONATE
pour
Flûte et Piano

FRANCIS POULENC (1957)

1 Allegretto malincolico

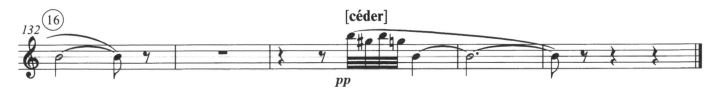

4

2 Cantilena

6

3 Presto giocoso

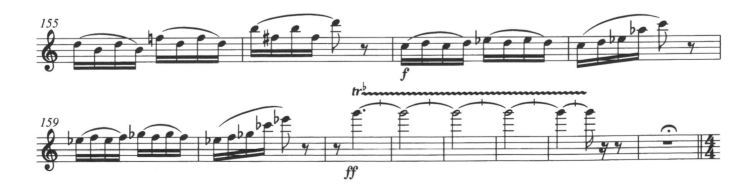

8

Subito le double plus lent [♩ = 66]

mélancolique

Tempo presto [Iº]

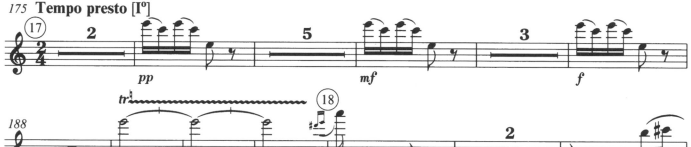

surtout sans ralentir

[Strictement en mesure et surtout sans ralentir]

Hotel Majestic, Cannes
Décembre [56]–Mars 1957

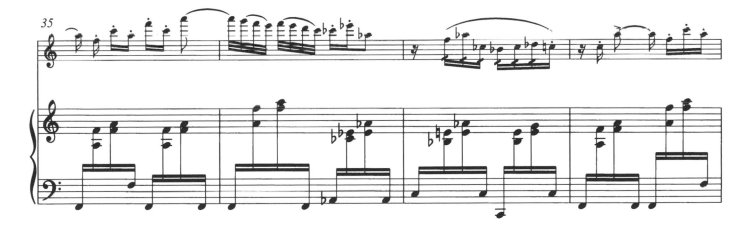

[surtout sans ralentir]

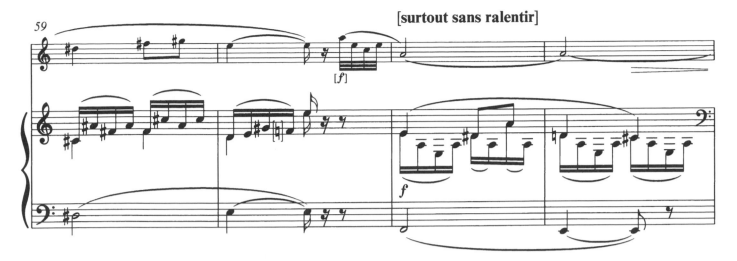

A peine plus vite [♩ = 92]

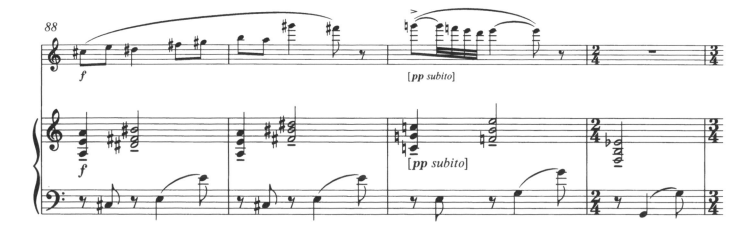

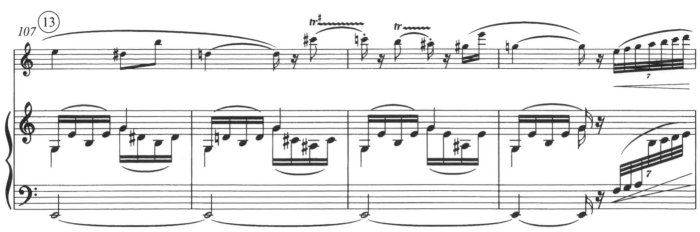

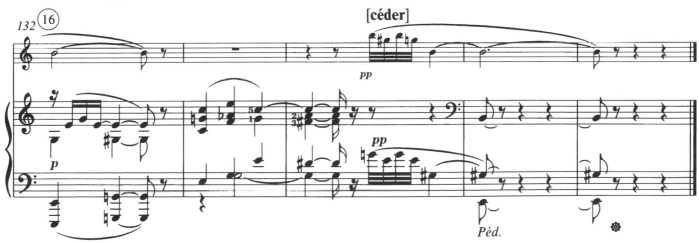

2 Cantilena

doucement baigné de pédale

3 Presto giocoso

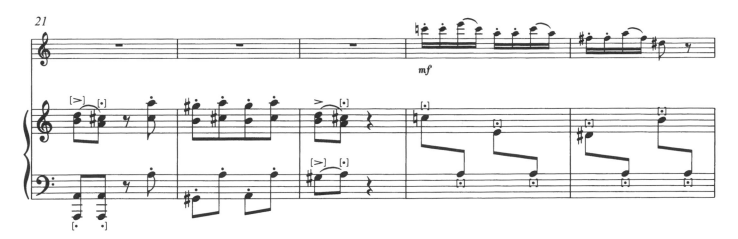

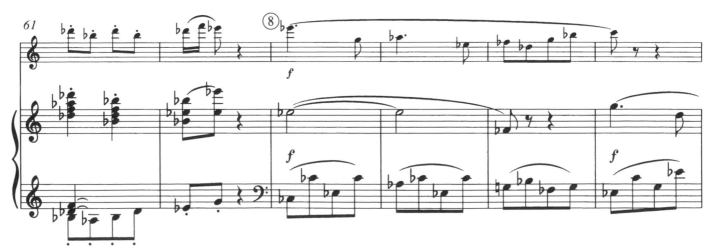

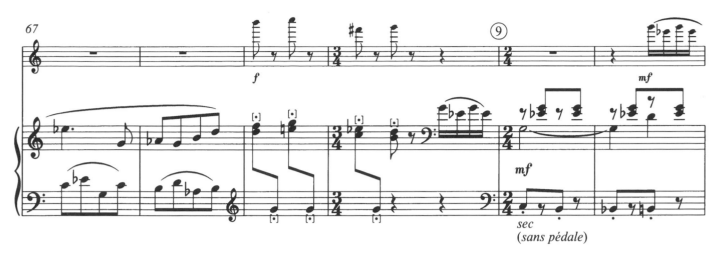

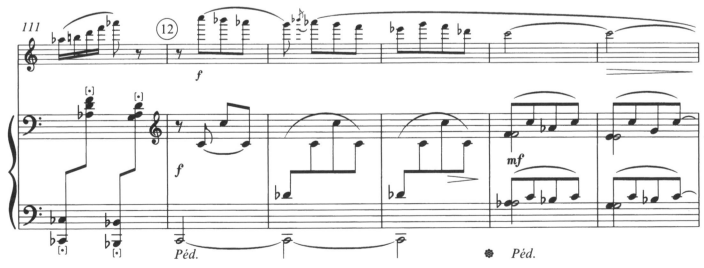

surtout sans ralentir

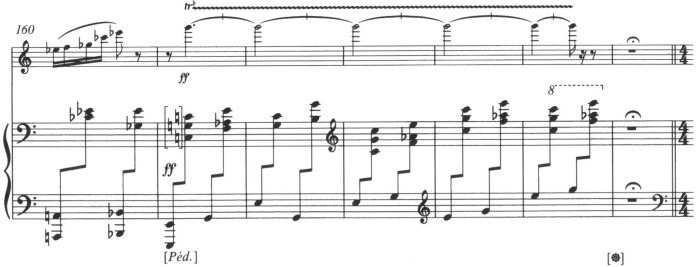

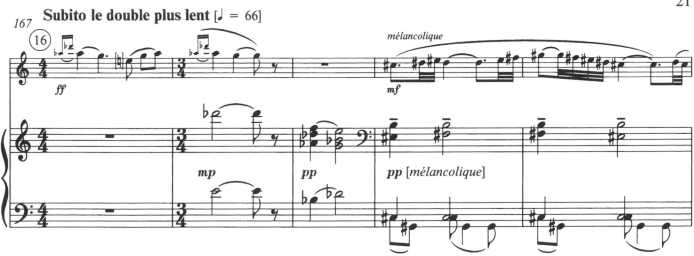

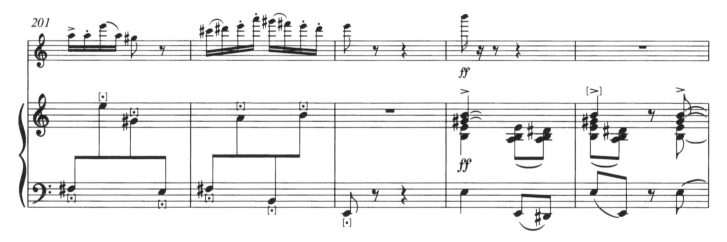

surtout sans ralentir

[Strictement en mesure et surtout sans ralentir]

Hotel Majestic, Cannes
Décembre [56]–Mars 1957

SELECTED MUSIC FOR FLUTE AND PIANO

J.S. BACH	Six Sonatas Bks. 1 & 2
BENTZON	Variations on an Original Theme
BERKELEY	Concerto (with Piano Reduction)
BERKELEY	Sonata
COOPER	Sonata for Flutes
DOPPLER	Hungarian Pastoral Fantasy Op.26
FAURE	Fantasie Op.79
FAURE	Sicilienne
LE FLEMING	Air and Dance
GODARD	Suite de Trois Morceaux
HEATH	Out of the Cool
HEATH	Rumania
JONGEN	Danse Lente
MACONCHY	Colloquy
MAW	Sonatina
NIELSEN	The Fog is lifting
NIELSEN	Fantasy Pieces Op.2
PREVIN	Peaches
POULENC	Sonata
SIBELIUS	The Oak Tree Op.109
VIVALDI	Sonata in C

SOLO FLUTE

BENTZON	Variations Op.93
BLAKEMAN	The Flute Player's Companion Vols.1&2
BOEHM	Twenty-four Capriccios
KOHLER	Progress in Flute Playing, Op.33, Bks. 1, 2 & 3
WESTERGAARD	Sonata